Surviving Education's Internet Revolution

Also from Westphalia Press

westphaliapress.org

Surviving Education's Internet Revolution

Vol. 3, No. 1 of Internet Learning

Edited by Melissa Layne

WESTPHALIA PRESS
An imprint of Policy Studies Organization

Surviving Education's Internet Revolution: Vol. 3, No. 1 of Internet Learning
All Rights Reserved © 2014 by Policy Studies Organization

Westphalia Press
An imprint of Policy Studies Organization
1527 New Hampshire Ave., NW
Washington, D.C. 20036
dgutierrezs@ipsonet.org

ISBN-13: 978-1941472958
ISBN-10: 1941472958

Updated material and comments on this edition
can be found at the Westphalia Press website:
www.westphaliapress.org

Internet Learning
Volume 3 Issue 1 Spring 2014

Table of Contents

Dear *Internet Learning* Colleagues,

I would like to take this opportunity to thank each and every one of you for your valuable contributions to *Internet Learning* this past year. We are already off to a productive start for 2014, and are currently working on the *Internet Learning Quality Matters Special Issue Fall 2014*. If you have not had a chance yet to do so, please check out our current issue (and past issues) for a multitude of exceptionally written articles covering an array of topics on online learning at http://www.ipsonet.org/publications/open-access/internet-learning

As part of expanding authorship and readership, I would also like to welcome several new members to our Editorial Reviewer Board. These highly distinguished scholars come from a variety of disciplines and also represent perspectives from a broader, international level of expertise—thus capturing topics around learning on the Internet on a more global scale. They include:

Paul Prinsloo, *University of South Africa*
Herman van der Merwe, *North-West University: Vaal Triangle Campus*
Ngoni Chipere, *University of the West Indies*
Tony Onwuegbuzie, *Sam Houston State University*
Molly M. Lim, *American Public University*
Clark Quinn, *Quinnovation*
Ben W. Betts, *University of Warwick, UK*
Tony Mays, *South African Institute Distance Education*
Robert Rosenbalm, *Dallas County Community College District & The NUTN Network*
Carmen Elena Cirnu, *National Institute for Research & Development in Informatics, Bucharest*
Mike Howarth, *Middlesex University*
Tarek Zoubir, *Middlesex University*
Jackie Hee Young Kim, *Armstrong Atlantic State University*
Hannah R. Gerber, *Sam Houston State University*
Debra P. Price, *Sam Houston State University*
Mauri Collins, *St. Rebel Design, LLC.*
Ray Schroeder, *University of Illinois Springfield*
Don Olcott, Jr., *HJ Global Associates*
Kay Shattuck, *Quality Matters and Penn State University*
Karan Powell, *American Public University System*
John Sener, *Senerknowledge LLC*
Melissa Langdon, *University of Notre Dame, Australia*
Kristen Betts, *Drexel University*
Barbara Altman, *Texas A&M, Central Texas*

Additionally, we have also added a new member to our Executive Editorial Board, Daniel Benjamin, who serves as the Vice President and Dean of the School of Science and Technology at American Public University System. With his extensive background in the field of distance education, he will undoubtedly offer a wealth of knowledge to *Internet Learning*.

Thank you once again for your commitment to serve and support *Internet Learning*. We look forward to your continued support with manuscript submissions, peer reviews, editing, copyediting, web and journal design, etc. and also welcome any comments or suggestions aimed toward improvement in these areas.

Warm regards,

Melissa Layne, Ed.D.
Editor-in-Chief, *Internet Learning*
Director of Research Methodology, American Public University System

This issue of *ILJ* consists of a selection of papers concerning different aspects of online teaching, learning, and quality assurance, stimulated by interaction with *The Quality Matters Higher Education Rubric* and course review process. It captures a small, but significant, sample of the kind of detailed analysis of online education toward which engagement with QM typically leads. This kind of work is advancing incrementally toward a better understanding of the most effective course design elements to promote learner persistence, performance, and satisfaction, as well as the most effective strategies to persuade faculty to adopt best practices and become part of the growing community of effective and committed online instructors and facilitators.

Why has the study of effective standards for online education grown steadily, beyond the usual confines of departments and colleges of education, in contrast to the level of interest in the higher education classroom? Of course, the Quality Matters™ Program would like to take credit for this trend, together with other organizations like ITC, WCET, MERLOT, and the Sloan Consortium, through our conferences, sponsored research projects, and activities to engage both faculty and instructional design and technology specialists. But something deeper is at work.

The process for online and blended course creation and improvement at the postsecondary level has engaged individuals and institutions in ways seldom experienced in face-to-face education. This work increasingly involves teams of individuals who need to share and collaborate in order to succeed. And the successful course, or even the well designed learning object, is itself an artifact that begs to be shared, analyzed and improved. This sharing begins locally, but spreads quickly to become regional, national, and even international. The collaborations that result from this phenomenon and the courses that are thereby strengthened, term by term, hold promise for the continual improvement of online education, year-by-year and version-by-version.

In historical terms, we are only at the beginning of this process. I suspect, however, that it will be a permanent feature of online education, leading to new strategies and tools, and, ultimately, a re-conception of advanced learning, individualized to the learner. It will also inevitably impact classroom-based education as well. We may be taking baby steps at present with studies such as these, but the baby (online education) is growing rapidly.

Ron Legon, Ph.D.
Executive Director
The Quality Matters Program
and
Provost Emeritus
The University of Baltimore

Collaborating with Faculty to Compose Exemplary Learning Objectives

Matthew M. Acevedo[A]

Inclusion of well-written, measureable, and student-centered learning objectives represents a major component in the Quality Matters (QM) higher education rubric. However, when an instructor-expert and instructional designer collaborate to create an e-learning product, oftentimes the instructor-expert either comes to the table with course and/or unit learning objectives that are already prepared, but are not measurable, student-centered, or aligned with planned instructional materials and strategies; or has no learning objectives at all. The responsibility then falls on the instructional designer to not only explain the importance of properly written learning objectives, but also to guide and support the instructor-expert through the process of composing learning objectives that are measureable and appropriate for the e-learning product. This paper discusses the purpose and importance of learning objectives and suggests several strategies for instructional designers, faculty trainers, and others who work with instructor-experts to compose learning objectives. These strategies are based on commonly encountered scenarios and are framed around a discussion of terminal and enabling objectives. These strategies also represent an alternative to the common practice of providing an instructor-expert with a list of Bloom's Taxonomy-aligned verbs, and can aid in successful collaboration leading to compliance with learning objective-related QM standards.

Keywords: learning objectives, faculty collaboration, higher education instructional design, Quality Matters

The collaborative process that takes place as a catalyst for the creation of an e-learning product, whether it is a higher education course, a corporate training module, or some other type of instructional digital object, is a unique one. Very often, two individuals – an instructor-expert and an instructional designer – are responsible for working together to design and develop the end product (Aleckson & Ralston-Berg, 2013), and e-learning courses in the higher education space are no exception. The relationship is unique as a result of the wildly varying backgrounds of the two parties – the instructor-expert is typically a scholar in a field unrelated to education, and a competent instructional designer is well versed in learning theories, instructional strategies, design thinking, instructional design process models, and uses of technology to promote learning.

[A] Matthew M. Acevedo, FIU Online, Florida International University. This article is based on "Beyond Understanding: Working with Faculty to Compose Exemplary Learning Objectives," a conference session presented at the Quality Matters' 5th Annual Conference on Quality Assurance in Online Learning in Nashville, TN on October 2, 2013. Correspondence concerning this article should be addressed to Matthew Acevedo, FIU Online, 11200 SW 8th St, Modesto A. Maidique Campus, RB227B, Miami, FL 33199. E-mail: mmaceve@fiu.edu

Further adding to the unique dynamic of this relationship is the idea that everyone, innately, is a teacher. In a recent webinar, well-known instructional design scholar M. David Merrill recounts a story in which he silently and patiently listened to his brother-in-law, a nuclear physicist, describe advanced and complicated mathematical derivations related to particle physics. Afterward, when Merrill began discussing his own work related to instructional design theory, his brother-in-law interrupted him and argued his points, feeling qualified to do so since "everyone is a teacher" (Merrill, 2013). The point is valid: parents and family members instinctively teach children basic skills and manners; friends may naturally teach other friends hobbies and games. Teaching and learning are part of the human experience.

A natural extension of this is the idea that faculty members may feel completely prepared to teach subjects in which they are experts or scholars. As a result, these instructor-experts may come to the drawing board early in the e-learning design process with learning objectives prepared, and, oftentimes, these learning objectives are not measureable, student-centered, realistic, or aligned with the planned assessment strategy. The responsibility then falls on the instructional designer to not only explain the importance of properly written learning objectives, but also to guide and support the instructor-expert through the process of composing appropriate learning objectives.

Learning Objectives and the Quality Matters Program

The Quality Matters Program is an organization dedicated to the promotion of quality assurance in online courses in the higher education and K–12 arenas through an iterative, faculty-centered peer review process. Quality Matters (QM) also emphasizes inter-institutional collaboration, faculty training, and implementation of research-based best practices in online course design. Courses that undergo the QM review process are evaluated based on a detailed rubric with standards for the course's learning objectives, assessment strategy, instructional materials, learner engagement, use of technology, learner support, and accessibility.

In a session at the Quality Matters' 5th Annual Conference on Quality Assurance in Online Learning, an audience of approximately ninety – mostly instructional designers – were asked to submit to a live poll via text message (see Figure 1 below); the prompt was "Working with faculty to compose learning objectives can often be…," and responses were enlightening. Typical replies included "frustrating," "maddening," "an uphill battle," "a challenge," and even "painful" (Acevedo, 2013).

Clearly, working with faculty to compose objectives represents a challenge for instructional designers, faculty leaders, faculty trainers, and others who work with instructor-experts in higher education environments. In this article, I will provide a framework, based on common scenarios, for collaborating with faculty members during the process of either composing new, or rewriting ineffective learning objectives. Additionally, I will include discussion as to how this process relates to the QM review process, since learning objec-

Working with faculty to compose learning objectives can often be...

ⓘ Start this poll to accept responses

"a losing battle, especially if the course learning objectives were developed by their department. The faculty feel they are untouchable. ."

"challenging and enlightening"   "frustrating"   "maddening"   "an uphill battle! Faculty often feel insulted."   "difficult"

"Exasperating because the believe that because they are an expert in their field is makes them an effort teacher. Lori"   "a challenge"

"like herding cattle"   "stressful"   "like eating banana bread WITHOUT nuts"   "frustrating"   "amusing"

"Maddening!"   "Frustrating!"   "exhausting and repetitive"   ". As faculty, talk to me not at me for these terms"

"irritating"   "_ lead to being bruised and battered"   "as if speaking a different language"   "a role reversal"   "painful"

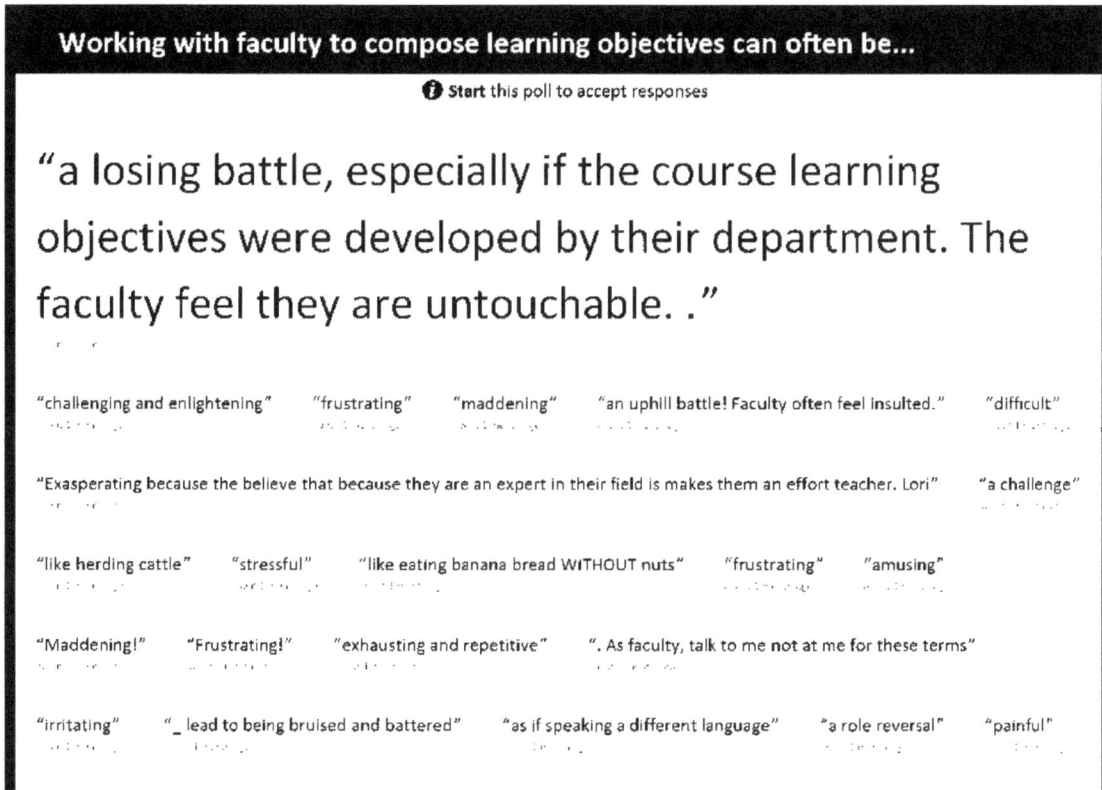

Figure 1. Sample responses from the text message poll.

tives represent a significant portion of the QM rubric.

The Importance of Learning Objectives

Robert Mager, likely the foremost classical authority on learning objectives, describes a learning objective as "an intent communicated by a statement describing a proposed change in a learner – a statement of what the learner is to be like when he has successfully completed a learning experience. It is a description of a pattern of behavior (performance) we want the learner to be able to demonstrate" (1962, p. 2). According to Mager, "When clearly defined goals are lacking, it is impossible to evaluate a course or program efficiently, and there is no sound basis for selecting appropriate materials, content, or instructional methods" (p. 2).

Learning objectives, derived from an appropriate needs analysis, serve as the underpinning to all well-known instructional design process models. According to Dick, Carey, and Carey, learning objectives "are an integral part of the design process […] Objectives serve as the input documentation for the designer or test construction specialist as they prepare the test and the instructional strategy" (2009, pp. 113–114). Furthermore, "objectives are used to communicate to both the instructor and learners what may be learned from the materials" (p. 114). Renowned educational psychologist Robert Gagné further elaborates on the importance of informing learners of the objectives in his classic text, *The Conditions of Learning*:

[T]he learner must be informed of the nature of the achievement expected as an outcome of learning. […] The purpose of such a communication to the learner is to establish an expectancy of the performance to be achieved as a result of learning. […] The primary effect of providing learners with an expectancy of the learning outcome is to enable them to match their own performances with a class of performance they expect to be "correct" (Gagné, 1977, p. 291).

Lastly, learning objectives are invaluable instruments in a climate increasingly focused on outcomes assessment and alignment with institutional, regional, and national standards.

Some, however, have expressed skepticism or disillusionment with the use of learning objectives. Rosenberg (2012), for example, questions the value of presenting learning objectives to students:

[D]o objectives truly help the learners? […] We've all been there; sitting in class while the instructor reads (or we view online) any number of statements, sometimes dozens of them, for each lesson or module, that often begin, "at the conclusion of this course, the student will be able to…" Each objective focuses on a specific skill or knowledge taught in the course, but may be too much in the weeds to answer students' bigger questions like, "Why am I taking this course?" "What's in it for me?" and "How will this help me down the road?" (para. 5)

Rosenberg offers that learning objectives don't offer students a sense of value in the course, and should be replaced (or supplemented with) a list of statements of expectations to "truly broadcast the value and worthiness of your training efforts" (para. 10). Rossett (2012) counters Rosenberg directly: "Marc, you urge us to add expectations to [learning objectives], expectations that assure links to work and results. I say that good [learning] objectives are themselves that statement of expectations" (para. 11).

Keeping in mind a terminal goal of a successful QM review, it will be assumed the learning objectives are, indeed, vital and foundational to the design of effective and quality instruction.

It should be emphasized that, despite their importance, learning objectives are of little value if not constructed properly. The most detailed, comprehensive learning objectives are framed using the "ABCD" model: audience, behavior, conditions, and degree. Audience refers to the targeted learners, behavior refers to what the learner is expected to be able to do after instruction, conditions refer to any setting or circumstance in which the behavior should occur, and degree refers to the acceptable standard of performance of the stated behavior. An example of an ABCD objective is "Given a right triangle with stated lengths of each leg, eighth-grade students will be able to use the Pythagorean Theorem to determine the length of the triangle's hypotenuse with 90% accuracy." In this example, the audience is "eighth-grade students," the behavior is "determine the length of the triangle's hypotenuse," the condition is "given a right triangle with stated lengths of each leg," and the degree is "with 90% accuracy."

In higher education environments, including e-learning, the ABCD framework might be overkill. The audience ("college students" or similar) is implied by the context of the institution or course and stating it would be redundant. The condition is typically also implied by the provided instructional materials and sequence. Including the degree element in higher education environments has the downside of declaring a less than optimal expectation (why

not expect 100%?). Mastery of the objective in college courses is typically assessed on a sliding scale (A through F). The behavior, then, is the most essential element of the learning objective. This is the element that is evaluated during a QM review, and it is also the most misunderstood and most misrepresented aspect.

QM Standard 2 requires learning objectives at both the course level and module or unit level that are student-centered ("The student will…" as opposed to "This course will…") and measurable. This measurable quality is the one with which faculty members often seem to have the most trouble. There are certain words and phrases that come up time and time again that are vague and immeasurable (see Table 1). The problem is not that instructors (and instructional designers) don't want students to accomplish these objectives; rather, these objectives cannot be assessed, because they are too open to interpretation, they are internal processes, or they are, by their nature, entirely subjective. Sound learning objectives should reflect measureable, observable, external behaviors that can be evaluated and assessed.

Working with Faculty

A common practice among instructional designers, faculty trainers, and others who are working with instructor-experts to compose learning objectives, oftentimes in preparation for QM review, is to hand over a sheet of paper with Bloom's Taxonomy and a list of measureable verbs that correspond to each level of the hierarchy. These lists are common on the internet and found easily with a basic search engine query. The designer or trainer informs the instructor-expert to reframe his or her objectives with these terms with no further explanation or conversation.

Understand	Learn	Know
Become acquainted with	Realize	Recognize
Internalize	Appreciate	Believe

Table 1. Commonly Seen Immeasurable Objective Roots

This practice (of which I'm guilty) presents a number of problems. First, without additional guidance, the list of objectives that is returned often doesn't mirror the planned (or existing) assessment instruments. For example, "Describe how controversies over constitutional issues shape much of the content of American politics" cannot be assessed using a multiple choice exam. Second, the level of cognitive complexity implied by the objective doesn't match the complexity of instructional content itself ("Evaluate the 50 state capitals" is an example). In some cases, verbs from these lists are chosen seemingly randomly.

Clearly, another approach – one that involves a more meaningful collaborative conversation – is necessary. This alternative approach excludes Bloom's Taxonomy altogether and starts with a conversation about the goals of the course and also provides a clear connection to the standards set forth by the QM rubric. Dick, Carey, and Carey (2009) describe two types of objectives: terminal objectives and enabling objectives. Terminal objectives are those skills that a learner will be able to perform once an entire unit or course is complete. Enabling objectives are subordinate to the terminal objectives; that is, achievement of a terminal objective is impossible without achievement of the enabling objectives.

In QM language, the terminal objectives translate to the course-level objectives, and the enabling objectives translate to the module- or unit-level objectives. An example may assist in illustration. Let us consider an overly simple course: "Foundations of Peanut Butter and Jelly Sandwiches." The terminal objectives of this course are:

Upon completion of this course, students will be able to:

• Select appropriate ingredients for a peanut butter and jelly sandwich.
• Assemble a peanut butter and jelly sandwich.
• Consume a peanut butter and jelly sandwich.
• Properly dispose of sandwich remains.

These terminal objectives, for the sake of QM compliance, become the course-level objectives. Each of these objectives have enabling objectives, or module/unit-level objectives. For example, the enabling objectives for the first terminal objective ("select appropriate ingredients") are as follows:

• Differentiate between different types of breads.
• Identify types of jellies and jams, including flavors appropriate for PB&J sandwiches.
• List the features of the different varieties of peanut butter.
• Describe accommodations for those with dietary preferences and/or restrictions.

It is also possible (and likely) that enabling objectives will have their own subordinate enabling objectives. For example, in order to "Describe accommodations for those with dietary preferences and/or restrictions," students must be able to:

• Explain the purpose of gluten-free bread.
• Explain the purpose of low-sugar jelly.

All of these enabling objectives become the module- or unit-level objectives, and can also aid in informing the organization of instructional content within a course. Skills that are necessary to perform the enabling objectives but will not be included in the instructional sequence or materials of the course are referred to as entry skills or prerequisite skills; these are requirements for learners before they begin the course of study. Refer to Figure 2 for a visual breakdown of these objectives and entry skills in the "Foundations of Peanut Butter Jelly Sandwiches" course.

Put simply, the conversation that needs to take place with the instructor-expert involves asking what, broadly, learners should be able to accomplish once they finish the course, as well as what learners need to be able to do, specifically, to accomplish those behaviors, including what will and will not be taught in the course. Based on this conversation, course and module objectives can be determined without bringing Bloom's Taxonomy into the conversation.

Practical Application

An analysis of terminal (course) objectives, enabling (unit/module) objectives, and prerequisite skills is a useful tool in working with faculty, but a QM review looks at courses, not at objective analysis in the wild. What does this breakdown translate to in "real life"? Figure 3 depicts a unit of the "Peanut Butter and Jelly Sandwich" course deployed in the Blackboard Learning Management system. This unit is framed around the first terminal objective ("select appropriate ingredients") and is called "Module 1: Selecting Your Ingredients." After a brief introduction to the module, the course objective addressed in this module is listed, followed by a list of that module's specific objectives. This layout is sufficient to satisfy QM Standards.

Common Scenarios

The typical scenarios faced by instructional designers and faculty trainers who work with instructor-experts to compose learning objectives can be categorized into five types. Each of these scenarios has a recommended course of action based on the terminal/enabling objective breakdown.

Scenario 1: Faculty member already has well-written, measureable objectives.

Given a scenario in which a faculty member or instructor-expert comes to the table with well-written, measureable, and appropriate objectives, the job of the instructional designer or faculty trainer is simple: commend the instructor-expert on the achievement, and provide any further support as needed. This scenario, however rare, does exist, typically with faculty who either have a background in education or have attended an *Applying the QM Rubric* training.

The remaining scenarios are more common.

Scenario 2: Faculty member needs help writing new course objectives.

In this scenario, perhaps the faculty member is preparing a new course or a currently running course doesn't already have objectives (obviously the latter is not the most ideal scenario given good instructional design practice). In either case, the recommended action is to ask the instructor-expert, "What can students do, after taking your course, that they couldn't do before?" The answer to this question leads to a discussion of the terminal or course-level objectives.

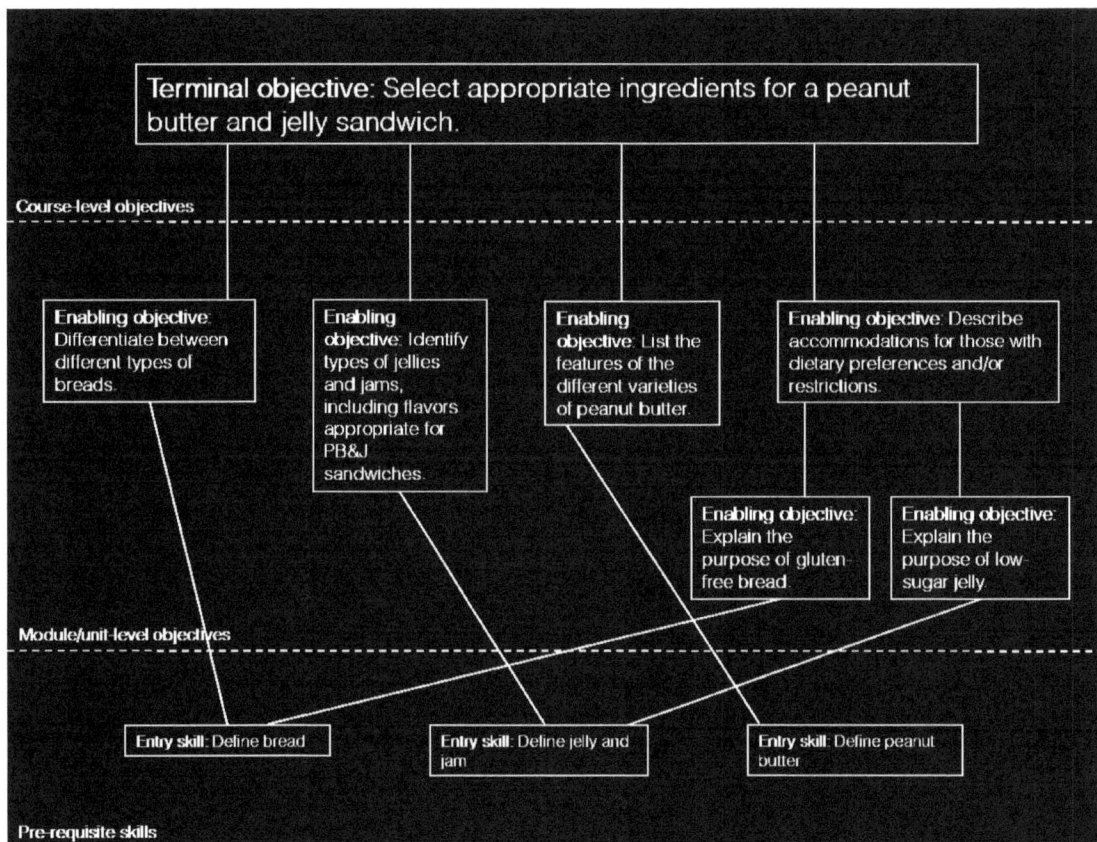

Figure 2. A visual breakdown of learning objectives in the PB&J course.

Module 1: Selecting Your Ingredients

Introduction

Welcome to the first module of Foundations of Peanut Butter and Jelly Sandwiches Im Prof Acevedo and I m excited to be your instructor for this delicious fully-online course In this module we re going to explore the different options that can go into your peanut butter and jelly sandwich You might be surprised how many options you have! We ll also take a look at some options for those with dietary considerations such as those who prefer a gluten-free or low-sugar diets

Learning Objectives

Course Objectives Addressed in This Module

- Select appropriate ingredients for a peanut butter and jelly sandwich

This Module's Learning Objectives

After completing this module you will be able to

- Differentiate between different types of bread
- Identify types of jellies and jams including flavors appropriate for PB&J sandwiches
- List the features of the different varieties of peanut butter
- Describe accommodations for those with dietary preferences and/or restrictions
- Explain the purpose of gluten-free bread
- Explain the purpose of low-sugar jelly

Directions

1 Watch the video from CHOW about choosing PB&J ingredients
2 Complete Assignment 1 Grocery Store Visit
3 Proceed to the Discussion Board to complete this module s discussion question "Crunchy vs Smooth"
4 Take the Module 1 Quiz

CHOW video: Choosing Ingredients

Figure 3. Course and module objectives used practically in the LMS.

Scenario 3: Faculty member has course objectives but doesn't have module/unit objectives.

In this scenario, perhaps the faculty member or instructor-expert has course objectives that are mandated by a department or program, or it's possible that the collaboration team has just graduated from Scenario 2. The recommended course of action is to ask the question, "What must students be able to do before accomplishing the course objectives?" The answer to this question will provide the team with the enabling or module/unit-level objectives. However, be sure to differentiate between enabling objectives and entry/prerequisite skills.

Scenario 4: Faculty member has some or all objectives that are immeasurable, vague, or "fuzzy."

This scenario is arguably the most common. Instructor-experts, as described earlier, often feel equipped to provide their own learning objectives with little or no background in education or sound instructional design practice. When an instructor-expert comes to the table with learning objectives that don't meet QM Standards, the recommended action is to inquire as to how that particular objective will be assessed in the course. If the answer is a multiple choice exam, chances are good that an appropriate verb for the learning objective is "identify." If the answer is fill-in-the-blank questions, more appropriate verbs include "recall," "name," and "recite." If the assessment instrument is an essay or a project, the prompt or instructions become the objectives themselves, although they may have to be generalized. For example, an essay prompt of "Compare and contrast the propaganda techniques of the Black Pan-

ther Party and the Socialist Workers Party" lends itself to an objective of "Students will be able to evaluate propaganda techniques of 20th-century revolutionary movements."

Scenario 5: Nothing else has worked. You've reached a "brick wall."

Some instructor-experts remain absolutely convinced that either their subjects are too abstract to warrant measurable objectives or that their immeasurable objectives are already suitable with no revision necessary. The recommended action in this case is to present the following situation: "Your student is going to work at an entry-level job in the area of this course. What is he/she going to do at work? What earns him/her a paycheck?" This doesn't necessarily give the collaboration team any direct answers, especially in liberal arts-type subject areas, but it can provide a jumping-off point or conversation starter to get on a productive and positive path.

Summary

The interaction and collaboration that take place between an instructional designer and instructor-expert tend to be unique, partially as a result of the widely varying backgrounds of the two parties, and can be somewhat complicated by the notion that part of an instructional designer's skill set is innate and can be performed solely by the instructor-expert. Part of this collaborative process can include the composition of course- and module/unit-level learning objectives, either (ideally) during the design phase or (less ideally) retroactively after the course has been developed. In either case, properly written, measurable, and appropriate learning objectives are vitally important because they provide students clear expectations, they inform the selection of instructional materials and instructional strategy, and they are used to develop assessment instruments.

When instructor-experts approach the collaborative environment without learning objectives or with learning objectives that are not measureable or well written, a discussion of terminal and enabling objectives is an effective tool for beginning the process or revising existing objectives. This approach is clearer and more direct than other methods, such as providing framed statements using Bloom's Taxonomy-aligned verbs.

References

Acevedo, M. (2013). *Beyond understanding: Working with faculty to compose exemplary objectives.* Concurrent session presented at the 5th Annual QM Conference on Quality Assurance in Online Learning. October 1–4.

Aleckson, J., & Ralston-Berg, P. (2013). *Mindmeld: Micro-collaboration between eLearning designers and instructor experts* (1st ed.). Madison, WI: Atwood Publishing.

Dick, W., Carey, L., & Carey, J. (2009). *The systematic design of instruction* (7th ed.). Upper Saddle River, NJ: Merrill.

Gagné, R. (1977). *The conditions of learning* (3rd ed., p. 291). New York, NY: Holt, Rinehard and Winston.

Mager, R. F. (1962). *Preparing instructional objectives.* Palo Alto, CA: Fearon Publishers.

Merrill, M. D. (2013, October 17). *My hopes for the future of instructional technology* [Webinar]. Retrieved from http://cc.ready-talk.com/play?id=2xrvdz

Rosenberg, M. (2012, July 12). *Marc my words: Why I hate instructional objectives* [Web log message]. Retrieved from http://www.learningsolutionsmag.com/articles/965/marc-my-words-why-i-hate-instructional-objectives

Rossett, A. (2012, July 12). *Why I LOVE instructional objectives* [Web log message]. Retrieved from http://www.learningsolutionsmag.com/articles/968/

Get Rid of the Gray: Make Accessibility More Black and White!

Erin Blauvelt

The Quality Matters Rubric (Quality Matters, 2011), a nationally recognized benchmark for the quality of the design of online courses, holds accessibility as an essential element of a high-quality online course. Creating and editing courses with accessible elements can be difficult, both in understanding and in process, as being able to interpret and administer the technical standards of Section 508 of the Rehabilitation Act of 1973 (1998) takes time and study. Customizing a definition of accessibility in online courses and creating the specific elements and best practices for an institution is essential in carrying out a plan for editing and developing accessible online courses and meeting the Quality Matters Rubric (Quality Matters, 2011). The purpose of this paper is to outline the process that Excelsior College used to establish an accessibility standards list and implementation plan to fit specifically with the course design and student population and to describe some best practices in coding and accessible design requirements to meet Standards 8.3 and 8.4 of the Quality Matters Rubric.

Keywords: accessibility, Quality Matters, online education, online course quality, best practices

Introduction

Laws, publications, and standards for web content accessibility exist for the purpose of assisting in designing accessible web pages for users with disabilities. Implementing the standards for web page design into an online course remains a "gray" topic and can be difficult to discuss and carry out in a "black and white" manner. The features of an online course, both technical and purpose, are different from those of a typical website, which most publications on web content accessibility exist for. It can be difficult to define what an accessible online course means to an institution and to move forward with a plan to be reactive and proactive toward accessibility. Excelsior College is currently completing a four-year project to make the entire library of 500+ online courses accessible as well as meet Standard 8 of the Quality Matters Rubric (Quality Matters, 2011).

Background Information

The Americans with Disabilities Act (1990), or ADA, which has been amended multiple times since its inception in 1990, outlines regulations and guidelines for providing equal access for persons with disabilities. Section 508 of the Rehabilitation Act of 1973 (1998) outlines technology-related regulations and standards for accessible web design. When students with medically documented disabilities request an accommodation during an online course, the institution is required to provide reasonable accommodation to the student. A reasonable accommodation adapts an exam, educational aid (in this case, an online course), or degree program requirement allowing equal access for an individual with a disability (Excelsior College, 2013).

In compliance with ADA mandates, Excelsior has a system in place for students with documented disabilities to receive accommodations for their online courses. This process is reactive in that students must first request an accommodation, and then the course is outfitted to meet their needs. In 2012, the decision was made to go beyond current federal laws and become more proactive in the approach to serve both students with documented disabilities and those that would also benefit from ADA-accessible course design principles, which is the concept of universal design. Universal design is a set of guidelines for the development of educational materials that provides all individuals, including those with disabilities and those without, comparable access to those educational materials (CAST, 2013). Individuals without documented disabilities can also benefit from universal design principles. For example, individuals with learning preferences (i.e., auditory or visual), environmental limitations (i.e., no access to speakers or a headset to listen to a lecture), and language barriers (i.e., English as a Second Language) reap benefits from universal design.

Excelsior College is pursuing institution-level recognition by Quality Matters and is currently in the second year of a three-year implementation plan. Accessibility is one of the eight General Standards of the Quality Matters Rubric (Quality Matters, 2011); thus certain criteria must be met in order to meet Quality Matters standards.

Accessibility Project Overview

The first two years of Excelsior's accessibility project have included creating a standards list, editing cascading style sheets (CSS) and Dreamweaver templates to meet accessibility standards, implementing a process to bring online courses in accordance to the developed standards list, and editing roughly 208 courses to comply with the developed standards list. A contractor was hired to assist in all areas of the project, but mostly for the purpose of serving as a co-subject matter expert and completing the bulk of the actual course edits. After developing a standards list customized for our courses (see Table 1), we edited institutional-level online course Dreamweaver templates and CSS for compliance with the standards list. The creation and implementation of the course revision process (see Figure 1) began once the standards list, templates, and CSS files were created and edited.

Developing an Instructional Accessibility Standards List

The first step in the project was to work collaboratively with the contractor to develop a standards list based on Section 508 standards (Rehabilitation Act, 1998), WCAG 1.0 Priority guidelines (W3C, 1999a), the design of and elements in Excelsior's online courses, and our specific student population. WCAG 1.0 includes three Priority levels, Priority 1 containing standards that content developers "must satisfy" (W3C, 1999b). Excelsior, serving mostly nontraditional adult learners, has a unique student population that would benefit from certain accessibility standards/universal design principles beyond WCAG 1.0 Priority 1 guidelines, so Priorities 2 and 3 were also considered when developing the customized standards list. For example, standards were added from Priorities 2 and 3, which address elements such as page organization and expanded detail of acronyms and tables with our high military student population (approximately 38% of our current student population) in mind. According to the American Council on Education (2011), individuals who served in Iraq and Afghanistan have up to a 40% chance of acquiring a traumatic brain injury. We can anticipate that there are more students with Post-Traumatic Stress Disorder (PTSD) and Traumatic Brain Injury (TBI) than have registered with our Office of Disability Services. PTSD and TBI sufferers typically experience difficulty with attention, concentration, and information processing (American Council on Education, 2011), so page organization can be important in their ability to absorb the content. Some Section 508 and WCAG standards do not apply to Excelsior's online courses, so the customized standards list was simpler than the Section 508 or WCAG standards lists. Upon establishing the standards list, Excelsior modified institutional course development practices to ensure that all newly developed and revised courses aligned with the standards list.

The Revision Process

This project is composed of continuously moving parts; therefore there existed challenges to arriving at a process that would account for periods of review, editing, and collection of materials – let alone sidestep the continuous tasks of preparing our online courses to run each term, implementing emergency fixes unrelated to this project, and normal course revision cycles. Excelsior College has regimented course development, course editing, and term preparation procedures and deadlines, which limit the amount of time a course may be out of commission for completion of accessibility edits. An additional challenge was

given of minimizing the time that we can ask of the academic units, who are responsible for managing the course content, as much as possible. The process outlined in Figure 1 was built toward the beginning of the project, and have had success with the tasks and order. Experimentation with the time span for each task and the number of courses in each task at one time has taken place. During the first year of the project, 101 courses were put through the process, with all of the courses moving through each task at the same time. This was found to be difficult to manage with only one staff member acting as Project Manager and long-term preparation periods when courses could not be edited. The decision was made to schedule courses in batches of ten, with a new batch starting the process every few weeks during the second year of the project, which was found to be a much more manageable solution.

As each course moves through the process, it is analyzed by the contractor using the accessibility standards list described above and submitted to the Project Manager in spreadsheet format. The spreadsheet is divided into items that the contractor can edit without any additional input, and items that need either Project Manager or academic unit input in order to be edited. The Project Manager first provides input that can be handed over without anyone else's involvement and then reaches out to the academic unit responsible for the course for input if needed. The Project Manager creates a clear list of input needing the attention of the academic unit and places a deadline for the input to be returned. Examples of input often needing the attention of the academic unit include creating alternative text for complex diagrams and tables and obtaining text-based versions of PDFs to replace scanned versions. After all input has been gathered, the course returns to

```
┌─────────────────────┐   ┌─────────────────────┐   ┌─────────────────────┐
│   1. AUs identify   │   │  2. PM prioritizes  │   │    3. C analyzes    │
│ courses for review/ │   │    and schedules    │   │     courses and     │
│        edits        │   │  courses for review │   │ submits results to  │
│                     │   │                     │   │         PM          │
└─────────────────────┘   └─────────────────────┘   └─────────────────────┘

┌─────────────────────┐   ┌─────────────────────┐   ┌─────────────────────┐
│    6. PM reviews    │   │    5. C completes   │   │    4. PM reviews    │
│ work and requests   │   │   edits and submits │   │      results and    │
│ additional work if  │   │    to PM for review │   │ provides requested  │
│       needed        │   │                     │   │   information to C   │
└─────────────────────┘   └─────────────────────┘   └─────────────────────┘

┌─────────────────────┐      Key:
│ 7. C presents final │      AU = Academic Unit
│   version of each   │      PM = Project Manager
│  course to PM for   │      C = Contractor
│      approval       │
└─────────────────────┘
```

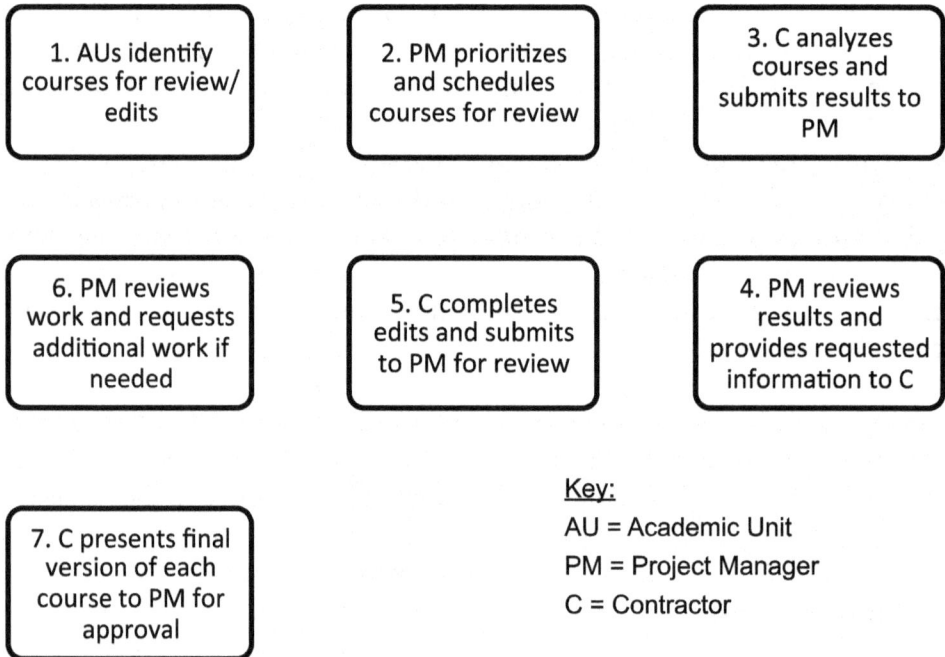

Figure 1. Course revision process.

the contractor for editing. Once editing is complete, the Project Manager reviews the course using the accessibility standards list and either approves the course or sends it back to the contractor for additional work if needed. If additional work has been requested, the Project Manager needs to review the course again for approval.

A goal for the second year of the project is to add staff members to the project to support the Project Manager, spreading out the work that needs to be completed, as well as the knowledge of online course accessibility in general. We also plan to implement the accessibility standards list into our course development process as soon as possible.

Quality Matters Standards 8.3 and 8.4

Quality Matters Standards 8.3 and 8.4 are both two-point standards, meaning that Quality Matters declares them as "Very Important" but not "Essential" (Quality Matters, 2011).

Standard 8.3 requires that "course design facilitates readability and minimizes distractions," which focuses on the visual aspects of the course. This standard most obviously affects students with physical impairments such as low vision or blindness, but it also affects those with cognitive disabilities, as their brains do not process visual elements in the same way that nondisabled students would. For example, while flashing objects can cause trouble for someone with a physical disability such as epilepsy, they may also be a barrier for processing anything else on the page for someone with Attention Deficit Hyperactivity Disorder (WebAIM, 2014). This standard covers elements such as the use of color, tables, graphics, text placement, and text format-

ting (Quality Matters, 2011). Table 1 provides some examples of common elements in an online course web page and some best practices to make each of these elements accessible.

While minimizing distractions does not mean that any design elements or images should be eliminated from online course pages, simplifying the design of the pages can make it easier for those with cognitive disabilities to process the page, or manipulate the page using an assistive technology program.

Quality Matters Standard 8.4 states "The course design accommodates the use of assistive technologies" (Quality Matters, 2011). Assistive technology refers to equipment or software that is used to improve or correct the functions of disabled persons (Assistive Technology Industry Association, n.d.). Assistive technologies can either be input devices that allow users to control and navigate computers and web pages, or output devices that interpret and/or manipulate data and elements on computers and web pages such as screen magnifiers, screen readers, and learning disabilities programs (Microsoft, 2014). A vision-impaired student may use an assistive technology like the screen reader JAWS (2014) to have the elements on the screen read aloud to them. A student with a cognitive disability may be much more successful processing the information when it is read to them by a screen reader or other type of assistive technology, and they may also benefit from being able to take the content on the screen and manipulate it, adding highlighting, breaking up areas of text, turning off images, or adding notes.

Standard 8.4 covers elements such as text formatting, equations, links, tables, scanned PDFs (portable document formats), and media (Quality Matters, 2011.) Table 2 provides some examples of com-

Element	Best Practices
Color	• Do not use color for instruction • Use only high-contrast colors together • Use color sparingly to keep the look simple
Tables	• Use tables to convey data in a simple, clean format
Graphics	• Include alt text tag with description of image for all essential images • Do not include citation of image in alt text tag • Avoid flashing graphics • Avoid animations that do not align with content
Text Placement	• Use <h1>, <h2>, etc. heading elements to convey headings and subheadings and order • Use bulleted and numbered lists where possible for simplicity • Break up large areas of text by chunking topics or using relevant graphics
Text formatting	• Use consistent font types and sizes • Do not use underline tag for emphasis, only for links (use bold and italics for emphasis)

Table 1. Examples of Standard 8.3 Elements and Best Practices

Elements	Best Practices
Text formatting	• Use <abbr> tag for abbreviations or acronyms • Use em for size instead of px (em is resizable, px is not)
Equations	• Use HTML codes for symbols when possible • If not possible to use HTML codes (complex equations), add equation as image with proper alt text tag of text form of equation
Links	• Use destination description as link title, not the URL • If link opens to PDF, video, audio file, etc. include file type and size
Tables	• Only use tables for data, not design • Use <caption> tag to describe table data • Use <th> (table header) tag to signify column headings
Scanned PDFs	• Find text-based version of PDF or scan a copy of the PDF (or original work) using an OCR (optical character recognition) software program
Media	• Provide text-only copies of media

Table 2. Examples of Standard 8.4 Elements and Best Practices

mon elements in an online course web page and some best practices to make each of these elements accessible.

Conclusion

Excelsior College is committed to offering accommodations to students with disabilities and assisting all students in being successful in their online courses. The Quality Matters Rubric (Quality Matters, 2011) holds accessibility as an essential element of a high-quality online course; however, creating accessible online courses and retrofitting existing courses for accessibility can be difficult. Careful consideration of specific institutional needs and online course structure, along with a structured implementation plan, can be helpful in administering the technical standards of Section 508 (Rehabilitation Act, 1998) into your online course program and meeting the Quality Matters Rubric (Quality Matters, 2011).

References

American Council on Education. (2011). *Accommodating student veterans with traumatic brain injury and post-traumatic stress disorder: Tips for campus faculty and staff*. Retrieved from http://www.acenet.edu/news-room/Documents/Accommodating-Student-Veterans-with-Traumatic-Brain-Injury-and-Post-Traumatic-Stress-Disorder.pdf

Americans with Disabilities Act of 1990, Pub. L. No. 101-336, §2,104 Stat. 328 (1990). Retrieved from http://www.ada.gov/pubs/adastatute08.htm

Assistive Technology Industry Association. (n.d.). *What is assistive technology? How is it funded?*. Retrieved from http://www.atia.org/i4a/pages/index.cfm?pageid=3859

CAST. (2013). *About UDL*. Retrieved from http://www.cast.org/udl/

Excelsior College. (2013). *Excelsior college disability services*. Retrieved from http://www.excelsior.edu/disability-services

JAWS [software]. (2014). St. Petersburg, FL: Freedom Scientific. Retrieved from http://www.freedomscientific.com/products/fs/jaws-product-page.asp

Microsoft. (2014). *Microsoft Accessibility*. Retrieved from http://www.microsoft.com/enable/at/types.aspx

Quality Matters. (2011). *Quality Matters rubric for higher education 2011–2013 edition*. Retrieved from https://www.qualitymatters.org/rubric

Rehabilitation Act of 1973, 29 U.S.C. § 794D (1998). Retrieved from http://www.section508.gov/section-508-standards-guide

W3C. (1999a). *Web content accessibility guidelines 1.0*. Retrieved from http://www.w3.org/ TR/WCAG10/

W3C. (1999b). *Checklist of checkpoints for web content accessibility guidelines 1.0*. Retrieved from http://www.w3.org/TR/WCAG10/full-checklist.html

WebAIM. (2013). *Cognitive disabilities*. Retrieved from http://webaim.org/articles/cognitive/

Continuous Improvement of the QM Rubric and Review Processes: Scholarship of Integration and Application

Kay Shattuck[A], Whitney Alicia Zimmerman[B], Deborah Adair[C]

Quality Matters (QM) is a faculty-centered, peer review process that is designed to certify the quality of online and blended courses. QM is a leader in quality assurance for online education and has received national recognition for its scalable, peer-based approach and continuous improvement in online education and student learning. Regular, robust review and refreshment of the QM RubricTM and processes keep them current, practical, and applicable across academic disciplines and academic levels. The review ensures validity in the set of quality standards that make up the Rubric. An overview of the regular review of the QM Rubric and process, as well as examples of the use of data to continuously improve the Rubric and process are presented. The guiding principles of QM – a process that is continuously improved upon and that is collegial and collaborative – are discussed in relationship to Boyer's scholarship of application and scholarship of integration. Glassick (2000) noted that Boyer's scholarship of overlapping discovery, integration, application, and teaching is "a hard but worthwhile task" (p. 880). This article outlines how the dynamic and rigorous processes adopted by QM continue to take on that worthwhile task.

Keywords: Quality Matters, course design, professional development, continuous improvement, quality assurance, rater agreement

Introduction and Background

The Quality Matters (QM) Program was initially developed under a 2003–2006 Department of Education Fund for the Improvement of Post-Secondary Education (FIPSE) grant. The grant, awarded to the not-for-profit consortium, MarylandOnline, was for the development of a replicable quality assurance program focused on faculty peer review and improvements to the design of online courses. During the grant period, a community of practice within Maryland researched, developed, imple-

mented, and disseminated a set of quality benchmarks (standards) (Shattuck, 2007), as well as a rigorous peer review process to improve student learning in online courses. In their wisdom, the developers of the QM program recognized that providing an instrument (a Rubric) and a process for using this Rubric would not be enough. Drawing from their own experiences as members of a community of practice that worked together for many years to solve the common issue of improving online course designs (Cervero & Wilson, 1994; Lave & Wenger, 1991; Schön, 1983; Cousin & Deepwell,

[A] Director of Research, Quality Matters Program
[B] Doctoral Student, The Pennsylvania State University
[C] Managing Director and Chief Planning Officer, Quality Matters Program

2005; Guldberg & Pilkington, 2006), they included required credentialing of specific competencies in the use of the Rubric and in an understanding of the application of the QM guiding principles of being collaborative, collegial, continuous, and centered in academic foundations around student learning.

Quality Matters is a program that subscribing educational institutions use within the cadre of other components necessary to assure quality in their online learning programs. While the QM Rubric[2] is focused on the design of online and blended courses, the QM process was developed with the awareness that it impacts faculty readiness through the QM professional training program (emphasizing pedagogical underpinning of course design), as well as the benefits of collegial interactions across academic disciplines and educational institutions. Other factors affecting course quality include course delivery (teaching), course content, course delivery system, institutional infrastructure, faculty training/readiness, and student readiness/engagement. The importance of other components in an institution's quality assurance commitment to online education is acknowledged within the QM standards.

Quality Matters is a faculty-centered, peer review process that is designed to certify the quality of online and blended courses. QM is a leader in quality assurance for online education and has received national recognition for its scalable, peer-based approach and continuous improvement in online education and student learning. As of the winter of 2013, there are 825 subscribing educational institutions and 160 individual subscribers; 3,998 courses have been formally peer reviewed; and 28,756 online educators have successfully completed QM professional development courses.

In this article, the QM guiding principles – a process that is continuously improved upon and that is collegial and collaborative – are discussed in relationship to Boyer's scholarship of application and scholarship of integration. An overview of the regular review of the QM Rubric and process, as well as examples of the use of data to continuously improve the Rubric and process are presented.

Scholarships of Application and Integration

While the construct of CoP (community of practice) (Shattuck, 2007) is useful in understanding the developmental phases of the QM program, the past decade can be described as an evolving practice of Boyer's (1990) scholarships of application and integration. In a seminal publication of The Carnegie Foundation for the Advancement of Teaching, Scholarship Reconsidered, Ernest Boyer challenged higher education to move beyond "teaching versus research" (p. 16) and for faculty to take on a scholarly approach to teaching by rigorous study of teaching in ways that are collaborative and connect theory with the realities of teaching. The term "the scholarship of teaching and learning[1] (SoLT)" is becoming an increasingly familiar concept in higher education (Hutchings, Huber, & Ciccone, 2011). Lesser known is that Boyer suggested "four separate, yet overlapping, functions" (p. 16) of scholarship. Those are the scholarships of discovery, integration, application, and teaching, and have been applied as useful tools in defining scholarship (AACN, 1999).

- The scholarship of discovery relates to the most traditional functions of research, that is, exploration to generate new knowledge.

- The scholarship of integration is *"inter-disciplinary, interpretive, integrative"* (italics in original) (Boyer, p. 20) and about "making connections across disciplines" (p. 18).
- The scholarship of applicaton is about use of knowledge from research to improve societal problems.
- The scholarship of teaching encompasses the relationship between teacher and student in which the teacher is also a learner to improve student intellectual growth

Boyer's call "to liberate academic careers from the hegemony of published research as the dominant product and measure of scholarship" (Bernstein & Bass, 2005, para. 41) served as a "tipping point" in the century-long debate of research versus teaching (Rice, 2002, p. 7). The growing sophistication of digital technologies of the past decade introduces new formats for the production, publication, and dissemination of faculty scholarship (Bernstein & Bass, 2005; Hatch, Bass, Iiyoshi, & Mace, 2004). The scholarship of application and integration is evident in QM's research on continuous improvement. Examples described in this article are

- Regular review and refinement of the QM Rubric and peer review processes;
- Consistently rigorous applications of the QM process, which are inter-disciplinary and integrative, and provide tools and strategies for interpreting research into useable processes; and
- Statistical analyses of data gathered during the QM peer reviews which inform continuous improvement of the QM Rubric and application of research and shared online teaching/designing expertise across academic disciplines and educational institutions.

Ultimately, the scholarship of teaching is behind the QM commitment to development and dissemination of standards of quality in online course design, which is a key phase in developing strong teaching presence. The scholarship of discovery – "disciplined work that seeks to interpret, draw together, and bring new insight to bear on original research" (Boyer, p. 19) – is the focus of QM's interest in original research. This interest will be the focus for 2014-2015.

Regular Review and Refinement of the QM Rubric and Processes

The 2007 article by Shattuck describes the development of the eight general standards of quality online course design as they were (and continue to be) informed by the independent research literature and established best practices. The QM Rubric and processes are dynamically interpretive of evolving research and best practices. The plan to conduct a complete review of the QM Higher Education Rubric and peer review process was established during the grant period, and reviews have become more thorough over the past decade. The ongoing history of review and refinement of the QM Higher Education Rubric and Processes chart outlines the review process and outcomes for the past five Rubrics, from the first to the current review.

The chart outlines the continuously improving processes used by QM to ensure wide input and transparency in the refinement of the Rubric and the peer review process. Figure 1 represents the current, rigorous, and comprehensive process followed to launch each new edition of the QM Rubric. The process is undergirded by the commitment to interpret research, best practices, and teaching/designing expertise into an applicable process that can be used across all academic disciplines. The collaboration of peer reviewers across disciplines points to Boyer's scholarships of application (practice) and integration.

Consistently Rigorous Application of the QM Peer Review Process

Following the principles of faculty-centered and continuous improvement, the QM higher education Rubric has been thoroughly reviewed and refined to ensure it remains a current and effective set of quality guidelines in online course design. It is important to recognize that while there is an openly accessible listing of QM standards, the full QM Rubric contains detailed annotations for each standard that assist in interpreting and applying standards during a course review. A course review without access to the complete QM Rubric and done by non-QM-certified reviews does not meet the rigors of the QM process. QM course reviews are conducted by a team of three certified QM Peer Reviewers (PRs) – all are active online instructors, all are currently certified as QM PRs, at least one PR is from outside the institution of the course under review, and at least one PR is a subject matter expert (SME) in the academic discipline of the course under review. Each team is led by a QM Master Reviewer (MR) who has extensive online teaching experience and in the QM review process, as well as having additional training in facilitating an inter-institutional virtual collaboration of academic peers.

Each QM PR brings at least two years of current experience teaching online. Additionally, each is required to complete rigorous QM training to become QM certified; each is subsequently added to the QM database of available PRs available to conduct QM course reviews. Each certified PR's academic discipline is included in the database. Course review teams are developed using the database of certified PRs. This ensures that at least one SME related to the course under review is included on each team. While a QM review does not evaluate the content of a course, an SME serves as a resource for others on a review team on any course design implications for a particular academic discipline. Each review team is chaired by a QM MR, an experienced reviewer with advanced training on the rubric and review process, who guides the team as needed in interpretation of the standards.

Consistent Application of QM Peer Reviews

Quality Matters is sometimes mistakenly described as a "Rubric," while in fact, it is a process of engaging online faculty who have further training in their use of a validated set of standards (encapsulated in the QM Rubric). This set of standards guides reviewers in their collaborative assessment of the design quality of a particular online course. The rigorous QM peer review process that results in courses meeting QM standards of quality (either initially or upon amendments) includes formal and informal reviews of online courses and online components of blended courses. Informal use of the QM Rubric is under the discretion of the subscribing institution. Formal course reviews are either managed by the QM program staff (QM-managed) or by certified QM representatives within a subscribing institution (subscriber-managed).

The analysis of 2008–2010 data found no difference between QM- and subscriber-managed formal course reviews in terms of total points ($t(272) = 0.831$, p $=.406$) or review statuses ($\chi^2(2) = 0.500$, p

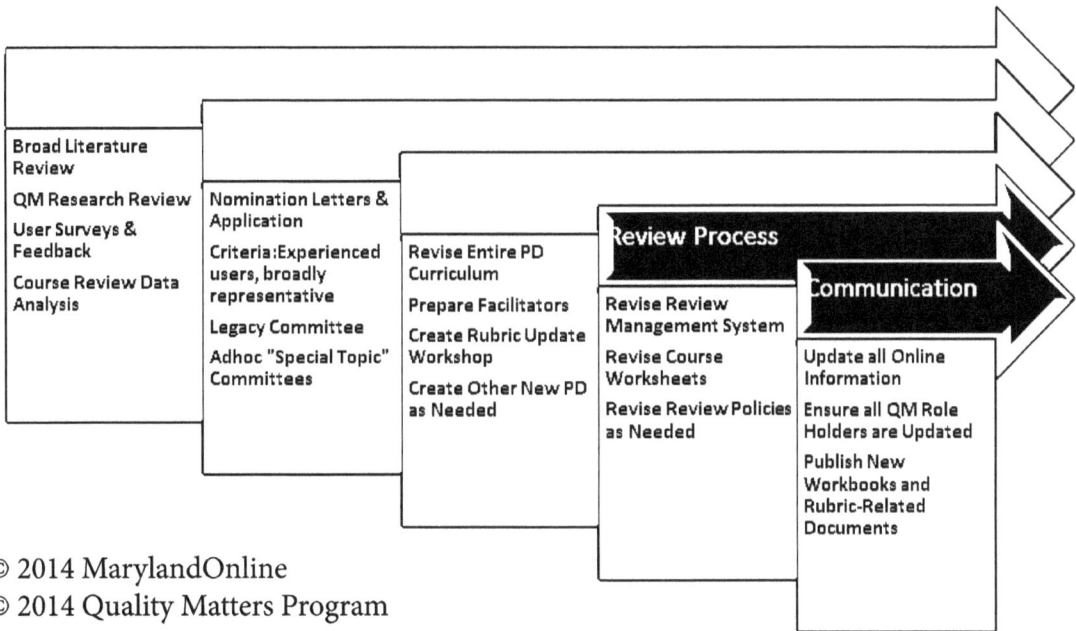

Figure 1. Steps in QM Rubric revision process.

= .779). This attests to the level of competencies provided by QM professional development required to become a PR and to the consistency of application of the inter-institutional, faculty-focused, peer-collegial review processes.

Examination of Peer Reviews 2008–2013

Statistical analyses were conducted on data gathered from formal course reviews conducted from 2008 through 2010 (n included 434 course reviews; of those, 180 were "informally managed") and from 2011 through July 2013 (N = 1,494). These data were explored to identify (1) frequency of courses meeting QM standards in initial reviews and after amendments, (2) most frequently missed standards, (3) differences between courses from different academic disciplines, (4) differences between courses submitted by faculty developers/instructors with and without familiarity with the QM, and (5) proportion of inter-rater agreement by specific standards.

Rate of Courses Initially Meeting QM Standards

In the technical report for the 2008–2010 QM Rubric (Zimmerman, 2010), the results of 274 QM- and subscriber-managed course reviews were analyzed. At the time of the data analysis, 39% (105) of courses met standards in the initial course review. An additional 48% (131) did not meet standards in the initial course review but did meet standards after an amendment. The remaining 14% (38) of course reviews were considered to be in the process of amendments.

In the technical report for the 2011–2013 QM Rubric (Zimmerman, 2013), the results of 1,490 course reviews were ana-

lyzed. At the time of the data analysis, 70.5% (1,051) of courses met standards in the initial review. An additional 26.6% (397) of courses did not meet standards in the initial course review but did meet standards after an amendment. The remaining 2.8% (42) courses were pending amendment.

Explanations of the increase in courses meeting QM standards during the initial peer review include (1) more courses are being developed using the QM Rubric as a course design guide; (2) more subscribing institutions are providing informal course reviews prior to submission for a formal peer review; and (3) more faculty and design teams have acquired effective competencies in the nuances of online teaching and course design.

Most Frequently Missed Standards

For the 2008–2010 course reviews, the most frequently met standards were 6.1 and 6.5; they were both met in 96% of course reviews. The standards most frequently not met were 8.2 and 3.5; they were not met in 54% and 60% of course reviews, respectively.

For the 2011–2013 course reviews, the most frequently met standards were 6.1 and 7.2; they were both met in 95% of course reviews, respectively. The standards most frequently not met were again 8.2 and 3.5; they were not met in 58.9% and 65.3% of course reviews, respectively. Note, for the analyses of the 2011–2013 course reviews, standards met in initial reviews versus amended reviews were not distinguished between.

Frequently missed standards are reviewed carefully by the Rubric Committee, as they might indicate the need for refinement of the standard and annotation wording or need for focused QM professional development for PRs.

Differences of Review Success by Course Discipline

Analysis of courses reviewed from 2011 through July 2013 revealed that business courses tended to have the best outcomes. Business courses were most likely to meet standards in the initial review, followed by education courses. Business courses also had the highest total scores. Courses in the remaining disciplines did not significantly differ from one another.

Relationship between Faculty Developer/Instructor of Reviewed Course and Familiarity with the QM Rubric

In the analyses of the 2011–2013 course reviews, courses submitted by individuals familiar with QM had higher initial scores than courses submitted by individuals who were not familiar with QM (Mann–Whitney U (N = 1,488) = 43,537, p < .001). However, there were not total point differences after amendment (Mann–Whitney U (N = 1,488) = 61,900, p = .108). (The amendment phase includes interaction with the peer review team.)

The familiarity of faculty developers and instructors with the QM Rubric was examined in relation to the outcome of the initial course review and the amended course review (when needed). In the analysis of the 2011–2013 Rubric, the majority (93.3%) of individuals who submitted courses for review were familiar with the Rubric. Only 98 out of 1,492 (6.6%) of individuals stated that they were not familiar with the Rubric.

Proportion of Rater Agreement by Specific Standards

Measures of reliability are often given when discussing scores such as those assigned using the QM Rubric. The term "reliability" refers to consistency of results. Inter-rater reliability is a measure of the relationship between scores assigned by different individuals (Hogan, 2007). In its strictest sense, however, inter-rater reliability works under the assumption that reviewers are randomly selected and interchangeable (see Suen, Logan, Neisworth, & Bagnato, 1995). This assumption is not met in the QM's process in which reviewers may be selected on the basis of their previous experiences or areas of expertise. The measurement of interest concerning the QM Rubric is the proportion of reviews in which all three raters assigned the same rating to a specific standard (i.e., all three reviewers assessed a standard as met or not yet met). This is different from inter-rater reliability in that it is not an attempt at describing unsystematic variance (see Hallgren, 2012; Liao, Hunt, & Chen, 2010); its purpose is to provide an easily interpretable statistic that will allow for the comparison of specific standards for practical purposes. Thus, in the discussion of consistency of results of QM's reviews, the term proportion of rater agreement is used as it explicitly describes the analyses performed as opposed to inter-rater reliability, which it technically is not.

One of the primary purposes of analyzing proportion of rater agreement is to identify specific standards that may require attention to keep the Rubric reflective of the research and fields of practice while being workable for a team of inter-institutional, inter-disciplinarian academic peers. A specific standard for which reviewers frequently submit different scores may lack clarity; this could result in the need for changes to the specific standard or it could signal a need for more reviewer training.

The standards with lowest rater agreement table provide an overview of the revisions made by the 2010 Rubric Committee for standards that statistically had the lowest rater agreement. The chart also provides data on the most recent data analysis and has been provided to the 2014 Rubric Committee.

Individual ratings given by a QM peer review in course reviews reflect, to at least some extent, that particular reviewer's professional/pedagogical opinion, and, therefore, may vary from the ratings of the other individual reviewers. However, markedly lower rater agreement for specific standards in the QM Rubric is a prompt to members of the Rubric Committee to focus attention on those standards during the regular review and refreshment of the QM Rubric.

Summary

Regular, robust (breadth and depth) review and refreshment of the QM Rubric and processes keep them current, practical, and applicable across academic disciplines and academic levels. The review includes interpretation of educational research, as well as an emerging emphasis on research generation. Expertise from online educators across the United States plays a critical role in the transparent, faculty-centered processes. The review ensures validity in the set of quality standards within the Rubric. Statistical analyses of data gathered from formal course reviews reveals that the peer review process has been consistently applied across review types and academic disciplines and points to the value of QM's professional development in which over 28,000 online educators have participated. The analyses also provide critical information to the Rubric Committee on the frequency of met standards and on the proportion of rater agreement by specific standards.

Glassick (2000) noted that Boyer's scholarship of overlapping discovery, integration, application, and teaching is "a hard but worthwhile task" (p. 880). This article outlines how the dynamic and rigorous processes adopted by QM continue to take on that worthwhile task. All aspects of the QM program are regularly reviewed and refreshed with and for online teaching faculty.

References

American Association of Colleges of Nursing, AACN Task Force on Defining Standards for the Scholarship of Nursing. (1999). *Defining scholarship for the discipline of nursing.* Retrieved from http://www.aacn.nche.edu/publications/position/defining-scholarship

Bernstein, D., & Bass, R. (2005). The scholarship of teaching and learning. *Academe,* 91(4), 37–43.

Cervero, R. M., & Wilson, A. L. (1994). The politics of responsibility: A theory of program planning practice for adult education. *Adult Education Quarterly,* 45(1), 249–268.

Cousin, G., & Deepwell, F. (2005). Designs for network learning: A community of practice perspective. *Studies in Higher education,* 30 (1), 57–66.

Glassick, C. E. (2000). Boyer's expanded definitions of scholarship, the standards for assessing scholarship, and the elusiveness of the scholarship of teaching. *Academic*

Medicine, 75(9), 877–880. Retrieved from http://www.academicpeds.org/events/assets/Glassick%20article.pdf

Guldberg, K., & Pilkington, R. (2006). A community of practice approach to the development of non-traditional learners through networked learning. *Journal of Computer Assisted Learning*, 22, 159–171.

Hallgren, K. A. (2012). Computing inter-rater reliability for observational data: An overview and tutorial. *Tutorials in Quantitative Methods for Psychology*, 8(1), 23–34.

Hatch, T., Bass, R., Iiyoshi, T, & Mace, D. (2004). Building knowledge for teaching and learning. *Change*, 36(5), 42–49.

Hogan, T. P. (2007). *Psychological testing: A practical introduction*. Hoboken, NJ: John Wiley & Sons, Inc.

Hutchings, P., Huber, M. T., & Ciccone, A. (2011). *The scholarship of teaching and teaching reconsidered: Institutional integration and impact*. Hoboken, NJ: Wiley.

Lave, J., & Wenger, E. (1991). *Situated learning: Legitimate peripheral participation*. Cambridge, UK: Cambridge University Press.

Liao, S. C., Hunt, E. A., & Chen, W. (2010). Comparison between inter-rater reliability and inter-rater agreement in performance assessment. *Annals of the Academy of Medicine*, 39(8), 613–618.

O'Banion, T. (1997). *A learning college for the 21st century*. Phoenix AZ: Oryx Press.

Rice, R. E. (2002). Beyond scholarship reconsidered: Toward an enlarged vision of scholarly work for faculty members. In K. J. Zahorski (Ed.), *Scholarship in the postmodern era: New venues, new values, new visions*. New Directions for Teaching and Learning, No. 90 (pp. 7–17). San Francisco: Jossey-Bass.

Schön, D. W. (1983). *The reflective practitioner: How professionals think in action*. New York: Basic Books, Inc.

Shattuck, K. (2007). Quality Matters: Collaborative program planning at a state level. *Online Journal of Distance Learning Administration, 10(3)*. Retrieved from http://www.westga.edu/~distance/ojdla/fall103/shattuck103.htm

Suen, H. K., Logan, C. R., Neisworth, J. T., & Bagnato, S. (1995). Parent-professional congruence: Is it necessary? *Journal of Early Intervention*, 19(3), 243–252.

Zimmerman, W. A. (2010). *Quality Matters 2008–2010 rubric report*.

Zimmerman, W. A. (2013). *Analyses of 2011–2013 Quality Matters Rubric*.

End Notes

[1] O'Banion (1997) focus on learning as a key concept of the learner-centered movement has become intertwined with the scholarship of teaching.

[2] While this article focused on the continuous refinement of the QM Higher Education Rubric, QM provides other Rubrics and accompanying review processes:

- K–12 Secondary Rubric (Grades 6–12), which, after the first regular Rubric review, is now in the second edition
- Higher Education Publisher Rubric

• K–12 Publisher Rubric
• Continuing and Professional Education
Rubric

Measuring Online Course Design:
A Comparative Analysis

Jiyu You, Sue Ann Hochberg, Phoebe Ballard, Mingli Xiao, Anthony Walters

This paper investigated the differences between students' and QM peer reviewers' perspectives of essential QM standards in three online courses. The results indicated that both peer reviewers and students share the same point of view in regard to evidencing the standards. However, they differed significantly regarding three of the essential standards. Factors that might cause the discrepancy are further discussed.

Keywords: Quality Matters, online course, design

Introduction

Online learning programs have grown tremendously over the last ten years. Best practices and standards for online programs and courses have been developed and implemented in higher education. To ensure the quality of online courses it is critical that online courses are designed according to a set of best practices or standards before they are delivered to students. Quality Matters is a faculty-driven, peer-review process that is collaborative, collegial, continuous, and centered in national standards of best practices and research findings in online and blended learning to promote student learning. It has been widely-adopted by higher education across the nation as a process and a rubric to continuously improve online course quality.

This study attempted to (1) validate the instrument design based on QM Standards to measure online course design; (2) investigate to what degree the selected courses meet QM standards from a student's perspective, and (3) identify gaps between students' perspectives and QM certified reviewers' perspectives about QM essential standards.

The results of this study indicated that most of the items in the instrument were designed according to the Quality Matters standards work to measure the design perspective of online courses. The results also show there are three tiers (Tier I: *to a great extent*, Tier II: *to a moderate extent*, and Tier III: *to little or some extent*) in regard to meeting the standards in the three courses.

The results on most of the standards evaluated in this study provided by both reviewers and students are the same, indicating that both peer reviewers and students take the same point view in regard to evidencing the standards; however, they differed significantly with three of the essential standards regarding course objectives, unit learning objectives, and grading policy. One factor that might possible lead to this discrepancy is that reviewers look for solid evidencing aligned with measurable learning outcomes while students look for clearly articulated objectives.

---

^A The University of Toledo

Literature Review

Student Perspectives

Several QM-related studies have been conducted with regard to student perspectives. These studies can be separated into two categories: a) student perceptions of the value of QM features in an online course, and b) student opinions about whether a course meets QM standards or not. Ralston-Berg and Nath (2008) stated that students value the same standards marked as *essential* "3" and *very important* "2" by QM, but value significantly less on standards marked as important "1" by QM. They further noted that students who claim to have high satisfaction in online courses also value all QM features over those who claim low satisfaction. Similarly, in Ralston's (2011) study results by rank of *importance* to students for success correlated with QM standards. Knowles and Kalata (2010) as cited in Shattuck (2012) stated that there might be a discrepancy in expectations between students and experienced QM master reviewers. They further offered possible explanations about this possible discrepancy--that students simply completed the survey without thinking about the standards and the course content or many of the design aspects that were clarified by the instructors during the course were being taught via channels that are not available to the peer reviewers.

Quality Matters Standards and Review Process

Quality Matters (QM) is a process and a rubric to continuously improve online course quality (Shattuck, 2012). It is a faculty-driven, peer-review process that is collaborative, collegial, continuous, and centered in national standards of best practices and research findings in online and blended learning to promote student learning. Quality Matters is a leader in quality assurance for online education and has received national recognition for its peer-based approach and continuous improvement in online education and student learning. The research-based QM Rubric is designed to evaluate only course design--not course delivery or content. The QM Rubric consists of eight broad categories broken down into 41 individual standards. These 41 standards can be used in a variety of ways ranging from providing guidelines for course development to the evaluation and certification of courses through an internal or external review process.

The goal of the QM review process is to continuously improve online course quality. According to Shattuck (2007), the process begins with a *mature* course, meaning the course has been offered for at least 2 semesters and the course instructor has revised it based on previous experiences. A review team with three certified QM reviewers who have online teaching experiences will review the course and provide feedback to the course developer. When conducting formal reviews, one of the review team members must be a subject matter expert in the field of the course being reviewed and one member must be a master reviewer. In the event that a course does not meet the required 85% (81 of 96 points, including all 21 3-point essential specific standards) constructive recommendations will be sent to the instructor/course developer. The instructor/course developer can meet with instructional designers to revise the course according to the recommendations. All courses reviewed by the QM review team are expected to meet the standards after necessary design improvements.

Statement of Problem

Research indicates that there are many factors that can affect online course quality. Some of these factors include course design, course delivery, infrastructures, learning management systems, faculty readiness, student readiness, etc. Course design is one of the critical pieces in the quality control process as it affects course delivery and the overall success of online programs. Quality Matters (QM) is a process and a tool to continuously improve online course quality (Shattuck, 2012). The 2011-2013 edition of the QM Rubric standards for higher education includes eight general categories with 41 specific standards addressing different aspects of online course design. Each of the standards is supported by rigorous independent online/distance research and designed by a team of experts in the field of online and blended learning. A team of three certified QM peer reviewers review online courses according to QM annotated standards and provide constructive feedback to course developers. Although QM peer reviewers are asked to assume a student's point of view when reviewing online courses there exists the potential for differing perspectives. Therefore, it is necessary to collect feedback from students about the course design.

This study attempts to achieve three objectives. First, it attempts to validate the instrument design based on QM Standards to measure online course design. Second, it attempts to analyze the data and understand to what degree the selected courses meet QM standards from a student's perspective. Third, it attempts to identify existing gaps between a student's perspective and QM certified reviewers' perspectives about QM essential standards.

Method

Instrument

Based upon the QM standards, an instructional design team developed a questionnaire that included 27 Likert-items questions (*to little or no extent* 1-5 *to a great extent*) and three open-ended questions. Feedback was also obtained from a professor in the field of research and measurement. The instrument, simply referred to as the *Online Course Design Evaluation Tool*, specifically focuses on the design aspect of online courses.

Data Collection

Student Data

Since fall 2011, the Online Course Design Evaluation Tool has been used at the university to collect feedback from students about design aspects of online courses. The project team identified three online courses for this project. One course was offered in fall 2011 and 35 students completed the survey and two courses were offered in spring 2012 whereby 18 students completed the survey in the first course and 20 students in the second course.

Reviewer Data

Three QM certified reviewers who were trained to review online courses from a student's point of view collected data and provided reports on each of the three courses; however, because this particular review was not an official review, none of the reviewers were subject matter experts in the field of study of these courses.

Data Coding and Analysis

To satisfy the first and second objectives of this study, data were collected from the three online courses and analyzed separately with Winsteps--a Windows-based software that assists with several Rasch model applications--particularly in the areas of educational testing, attitude surveys and rating scale analysis (Linacre, J. M., 2009).

To address the third objective of this project the resulting data were treated. Students' results were converted into a measure that is comparable to the reviewers' rating. Student responses of *to a great extent* "4" or *to a very great extent* "5" are used as at or above 85% level and coded as "1". Student responses of *to a moderate extent* "3", *to some extent* "2" and *to little or no extent* "1" are used as below 85% level and coded as "0". According to the majority rule principle, if 2/3 of the students selects *to a great extent* "4" or *to a very great extent* "5" for an item in the survey then it is determined that the course meets that specific standard from a student's perspective. See Tables 1, 2, and 3.

Three QM certified peer reviewers reviewed the three courses according to QM standards and input their scores into a spreadsheet. If a standard was met, "1" was recorded for the standard. If a standard was not met, "0" was recorded for the standard. If two (2/3) of the peer reviewers assigned a score to a specific standard, then it was determined that the course met the standard from a peer reviewer's perspective. See Tables 1, 2, and 3.

The data were treated in a spreadsheet and analyzed with SPSS. A nonparametric Mann-Whitney U test (2 independent samples) was used to evaluate median differences between the two groups (students and peer reviewers). Although the peer reviewers were asked to take a student's point of view, the two groups were independent.

Results

Course A

Thirty-five out of the 44 students completed the course design evaluation survey with a response rate of 79.55%. The person reliability was 0.83 and the item reliability was 0.48.

The item statistics indicate that Item 1 (MNSQ = 3.31) will need to be revised and Item 16 (MNSQ = 3.13) will need to be revised or dropped if the instrument is used in the future.

The Item Map (Fig. 1) indicates that there are three tiers regarding course quality from a student's persepctive. Tier I contains the items that students strongly agreed with, thus indicating the course met Standards 2.1 (Item 4), 3.1 (Item 14), 3.2 (Item 15), 6.1 (Item 20), 3.3 (Item 7) to a great extent. Tier II contains items that students agreed with, which indicates that course met those standatds to a moderate extent. Tier III contains items that students agreed with to some extent, thus indicating that the course did not meet Standards 7.1 (Item 24), 5.1 (Item 13), and 8.1 (Item 25).

Course B

Eighteen out of the 38 students completed the course design evaluation survey with a response rate of 47.37%. The person reliability was 0.95 and the item reliability is 0.63.

The item statistics indicate that Item 14 (MNSQ = 2.29) needs to be revised if the instrument is used in the future.

The Item Map (Fig. 2) indicates that there are three tiers regarding course

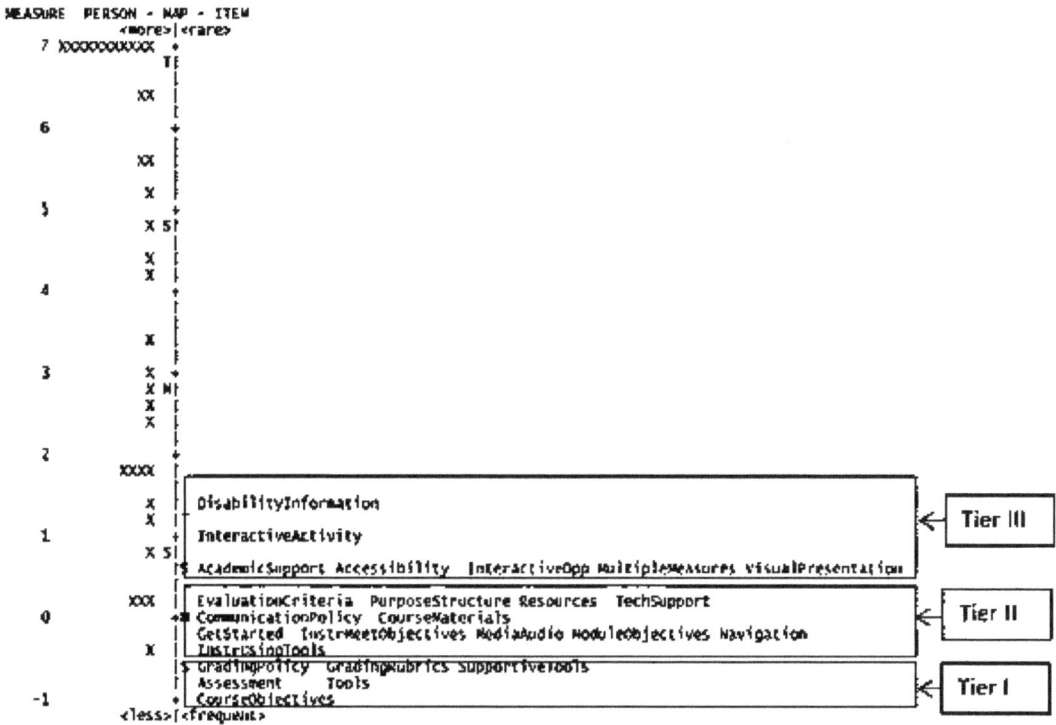

Figure 1. Course A item map

quality from a student's persepctive. Tier I contains the items that students strongly agreed with, which indicates the course met Standards 3.3 (Item 7), 3.2 (Item 15), 3.2 (Item 15) to a great extent. Tier II contains the items that students agreed with, thereby indicating that the course met these standards to a moderate extent. Tier III contains items that students agreed with to some extent, thus indicating that the course did not meet Standards 7.2 (Item 24) and 8.1 (Item 25).

Course C

Twenty out of the 22 students completed the course design evaluation survey with a response rate of 90.91%. The person reliability was 0.96 and the item reliability was 0.78.

The item statistics indicate that Item 10 (MNSQ = 2.83) will be dropped and Item 12 (MNSQ = 2.64) and Item 6 (MNSQ = 2.60) will need to be revised if the instrument is used in the future.

The Item Map (Fig. 3) indicates that there are three tiers regarding course quality from a student's persepctive. Tier I contains the item that students strongly agreed with, indicating the course met Standard 2.2 (Item 5) to a great extent. Tier II contains the items that students agreed with, thus showing that the course met these standards to a moderate extent. Tier III contains the item that students agreed to some extent, demonstrating that the course did not meet Standard (Item 10), a non-essential standard.

To satisfy the third objective of this project the data were treated as follows:

• Students' results were converted into a measure comparable to that of the reviewers' rating. Student responses of *to a great extent* "4" or *to a very great extent* "5" were used as at or above 85% level and coded as "1". Student responses of *to a moderate extent* "3", *to some extent* "2" and *to little or no extent* "1" were used as below 85% level and coded as "0". According to the majority rule principle if 2/3 of the students selects *to a great extent* "4" or *to a very great extent* "5" for an item in the survey then it was determined that the course met that particular standard from a student's perspective. See Tables 1, 2, and 3.

• Three QM certified peer reviewers reviewed the three courses according to QM standards and recorded their scores in a spreadsheet. If a standard was met, "1" was recorded for the standard. If a standard was not met, "0" was recorded for the standard. If two (2/3) of the peer reviewers assigned a score to a specific standard then the course met that standard from a peer reviewer's perspective. See Tables 1, 2, and 3.

The data were treated in a spreadsheet and analyzed with SPSS. A nonparametric Mann-Whitney U test (2 independent samples) was used to evaluate a difference in medians between the two groups (students and peer reviewers). The two groups were different and independent of each other even though peer reviewers are asked to take a student's view when completing course reviews.

```
MEASURE PERSON - MAP - ITEM
        <more>|<rare>
  7       X  +
           T|
           |
           |
  6       X +
          X +
          X +
  5         +
           |
       XX S|
  4         +
           |
           |
  3       X +
         XX  |
          X  |M
         XX +
  2      XX +   Dtsubilityinformation
           |
          X +
           |T
  1         +   Accessibility
           |
        S|S InteractiveActivity  TechSupport  Tools
           |   AcademicSupport      Navigation
           |   MultipleMeasures
        X |M Assessment           GetStarted  InstrMeetObjectives InstrUsingTools
  0       X +   ModuleObjectives
        X |   CommunicationPolicy  InteractiveOpp SupportiveTools
           |   CourseMaterials      CourseObjectives
        X |   PurposeStructure
 -1        |S EvaluationCriteria   GradingPolicy MediaAudio VisualPresentation
           |   Resources
           |T  GradingRubrics
           |t
 -2        +
       <less>|<frequent>
```

Tier III

Tier II

Tier I

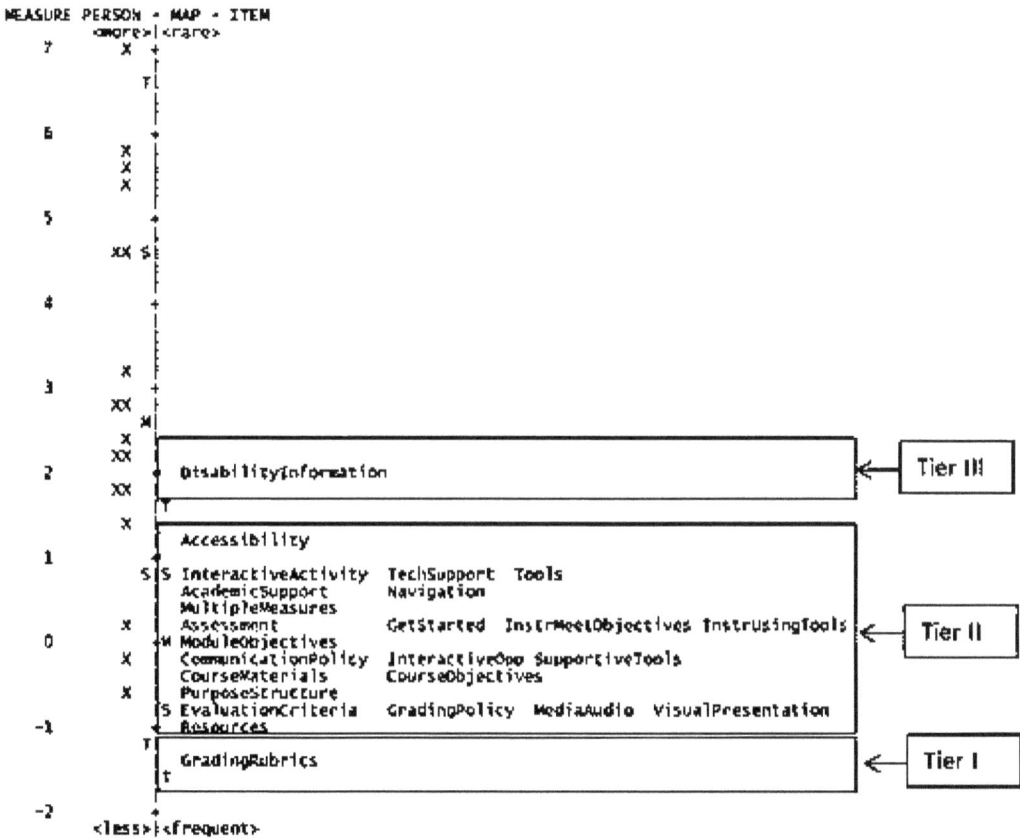

Figure 2. Course B item map

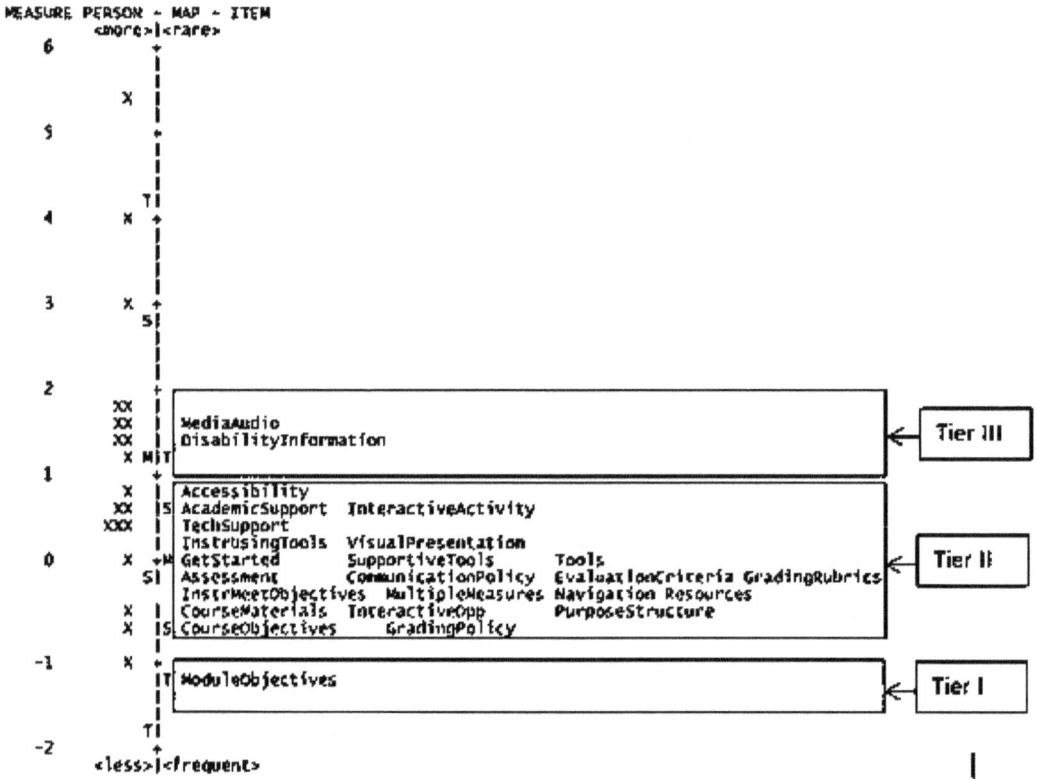

Figure 3. Course C item map

Course A

Students reported that the course met all of the essential standards except Standards 7.1, 7.2, and 8.1 as measured by the instrument developed by the research team. The review results conducted by the three certified peer reviewers (none of the peer reviewers served as an SME on this review) also indicate that the course met most of the essential standards except Standards 2.1, 2,2, 2.4, 3.3, and 8.1.

Table 1 Student and Peer Reviewer Results on the Essential Standards

Essential Standards	Student Results	Peer Reviewer Results	Items
1.1	YES	YES	2
1.2	YES	YES	1
2.1	YES	NO	4
2.2	YES	NO	5
2.4	YES	NO	6
3.1	YES	YES	14
3.2	YES	YES	15
3.3	YES/YES	NO	7, 16
4.1	YES	YES	8
5.1	YES	YES	13
5.2	YES	YES	12
6.1	YES	YES	20
6.3	YES	YES	21
7.1	NO	YES	22
7.2	NO	YES	24
8.1	NO	NO	25

No statistical differences were detected regarding the standards, with the exception of Standards 2.1, 2.4, and 3.3. The two groups differed significantly regarding Standard 2.1 $U = 1.000$, $Z = -5.192$, $p = .000$, Standard 2.4 $U = 7.500$, $Z = -3.393$, $p = .001$, and Standard 3.3 (Item 7) $U = 22.000$, $Z = -2.819$, $p = .005$. See Fig. 4 below.

Test Statistics[b]

	S2.1	S2.2	S2.4	S3.3A	S4.1
Mann-Whitney U	1.500	23.500	7.500	22.000	43.500
Wilcoxon W	7.500	29.500	13.500	28.000	673.500
Z	-5.192	-2.485	-3.393	-2.819	-.771
Asymp. Sig. (2-tailed)	.000	.013	.001	.005	.441
Exact Sig. [2*(1-tailed Sig.)]	.000[a]	.122[a]	.008[a]	.109[a]	.644[a]

a. Not corrected for ties.

b. Grouping Variable: Role

Figure 4. Mann-Whitney U test statistics

Course B

Students reported that the course met all of the essential standards except Standards 7.1, 7.2 and 8.1 as measured by the Online Course Evaluation Tool; however, the review results conducted by the three certified peer reviewers (none of the peer reviewers served as an SME on this review) indicated that at least five course essential Standards 1.1, 1.2, 2.2, 2.4 and 3.2 did not meet the standards. Similarly, the peer reviewers' results indicated that the course did not meet Standards 7.1, 7.2, and 8.1, however, interestingly, the students disagreed with that decision.

Table 2 Student and Peer Reviewer Results on the Essential Standards

Essential Standards	Student Results	Peer Reviewer Results	Items
1.1	YES	NO	2
1.2	YES	NO	1
2.1	YES	YES	4
2.2	YES	NO	5
2.4	YES	NO	6
3.1	YES	YES	14
3.2	YES	NO	15
3.3	YES/YES	YES	7, 16
4.1	YES	YES	8
5.1	YES	YES	13
5.2	YES	YES	12
6.1	YES	YES	20
6.3	YES	YES	21
7.1	NO	YES	22
7.2	NO	YES	24
8.1	NO	YES	25

No statistical differences were detected regarding the standards with the execption of Standards 2.2, and 3.2. The two groups differed significantly regarding Standard 2.2 $U = 4.500, Z = -2.887, p = .004$, and Standard 3.2 $U = 3.000, Z = -3.266, p = .001$. See Fig. 5 below.

Test Statistics[b]

	S1.2	S5.2	S5.1	S3.1	S3.2	S3.3B
Mann-Whitney U	12.000	21.000	19.500	25.500	3.000	22.500
Wilcoxon W	18.000	192.000	172.500	31.500	9.000	193.500
Z	-2.214	-.886	-.916	-.192	-3.266	-.745
Asymp. Sig. (2-tailed)	.027	.376	.360	.847	.001	.456
Exact Sig. [2*(1-tailed Sig.)]	.153[a]	.600[a]	.546[a]	.887[a]	.011[a]	.669[a]

a. Not corrected for ties.

b. Grouping Variable: Role

Figure 5. Mann-Whitney test statistics

Test Statistics[b]

	S2.1	S2.2	S2.4	S3.3A	S4.1
Mann-Whitney U	24.000	4.500	16.500	24.000	19.500
Wilcoxon W	195.000	10.500	22.500	195.000	190.500
Z	-.592	-2.887	-1.291	-.592	-1.021
Asymp. Sig. (2-tailed)	.554	.004	.197	.554	.307
Exact Sig. [2*(1-tailed Sig.)]	.814[a]	.017[a]	.307[a]	.814[a]	.471[a]

a. Not corrected for ties.

b. Grouping Variable: Role

Figure 6. Mann-Whitney test statistics

Course C

Students reported that the course met only a few essential standards 1.2, 2.1, 2.2, 2.4, 3.2, 4.1, and 5.2. However, the review results conducted by the three certified peer reviewers (none of the peer reviewers served as an SME on this review) indicated that only three of the essential standards were not met, standards 2.2, 7.2 and 8.1. The peer reviewers' results for standards 7.2 and 8.1 are in conformity with the students' results that the course does not meet these standards.

Table 3 Student and Peer Reviewer Results for the Essential Standards

Essential Standards	Student Results	Peer Reviewer Results	Items (see the instrument for questions)
1.1	NO	YES	2
1.2	YES	YES	1
2.1	YES	YES	4
2.2	YES	NO	5
2.4	YES	YES	6
3.1	NO	YES	14
3.2	YES	YES	15
3.3	NO/YES	YES	7, 16
4.1	YES	YES	8
5.1	NO	YES	13
5.2	YES	YES	12
6.1	NO	YES	20
6.3	NO	YES	21
7.1	NO	YES	22
7.2	NO	NO	24
8.1	NO	NO	25

No statistical differences were detected regarding the standards except Standard 2.2. The two groups differed significantly regarding Standard 2.2 $U = 11.500$, $Z = -2.892$, $p = .004$. See

Test Statistics[b]

	S2.1	S2.2	S2.4	S3.3A	S4.1
Mann-Whitney U	22.500	11.500	21.000	19.500	21.000
Wilcoxon W	232.500	17.500	231.000	229.500	231.000
Z	-.957	-2.892	-1.079	-1.202	-1.079
Asymp. Sig. (2-tailed)	.338	.004	.280	.230	.280
Exact Sig. [2*(1-tailed Sig.)]	.514[a]	.094[a]	.457[a]	.355[a]	.457[a]

a. Not corrected for ties.

b. Grouping Variable: Role

Figure 7. Mann-Whitney U test statistics

Discussion

We investigated the differences between students and peer reviewers regarding the essential standards in three online courses. When the courses were approved for design the faculty course developers were provided a copy of the Quality Matters Rubrics in the beginning of the course development process. Instructional designers, who were certified QM peer reviewers, were available for individual consultations during the design and development process. The faculty course developers were very familiar with the standards and agreed that it was essential to incorporate the standards into online course design processes.

As reported in the results section, in course A the results reported by students and peer reviewers differed significantly in regards to Standard 2.1 (*The course learning objectives describe outcomes that are measurable*) and Standard 2.4 (*Instructions to students on how to meet the learning objectives are adequate and stated clearly*). For Standard 2.1, the students were asked to report whether course objectives were clearly presented in the course syllabus. For Standard 2.4, both reviewers and students were asked to report whether clear instructions on how students should meet the learning objectives are articulated in the course. Students reported that the instructions were available. However, reviewers do not agree as one stated:

> Standard 2.4 calls for clear instructions on how students should meet the learning objectives. The course design does a good job in providing students with a brief introduction to each Chapter topic; however, it is somewhat difficult to understand which learning activities, resources, assignments, and assessments support the learning objectives for each unit week. It is important to help students connect the

dots between chapter level objectives and the assigned activities and assessment for the week.

Apparently peer reviewers are looking for above average at approximately 85%. Students might think the brief introduction to each chapter provides instructions on how to achieve the learning objectives. The overall satisfaction of the course might also affect students' rating on the standards as the majority rated the course as excellent. A third factor that might contribute to the difference is the student satisfaction of the teacher. The responses to the open-ended questions indicated that the professor was excellent and cares about student learning, as one student stated:

> The professor always leads a very informative, fun, and creative class and this one was not an exception. I learned a plethora of new things from the reading, assignments, and independent studies throughout the semester.

In course B the results reported by students and peer reviewers differed significantly regarding Standard 2.2 (*The module/unit learning objectives describe outcomes that are measurable and consistent with the course-level objectives*) and Standard 3.2 (*The course grading policy is stated clearly*). For Standard 2.2, the students were asked to report whether module/unit objectives were clearly stated in each unit. For Standard 3.2, both reviewers and students were asked to report whether grading policy was clearly articulated in the course. Students reported that the grading policy was available, however, the majority of the reviewers thought that the policy was not clear enough. One reviewer stated:

> Standard 3.2 asks for a clear, written description on how student's grades will be calculated, for instance, the total points for each assignment, the percentages or weights for each component of the course

grade. It would be helpful to provide an overall list of assignments, points, percentages or weights in the syllabus so that students are acknowledged upfront on how they will be evaluated without digging deeper in the Unit content pages.

As mentioned previously, the overall satisfaction of the course and the instructor might also affect students' rating on the standards as students stated:

> Overall, this course has given me a lot of valuable information that I can use in the classroom.

> I appreciate all the help given to me throughout the years. This was not an easy thing to accomplish, but I have and I will always remember all those that have helped me succeed.

In course C the results reported by students and peer reviewers differed significantly in regards to Standard 2.2 (*The module/unit learning objectives describe outcomes that are measurable and consistent with the course-level objectives*). The students were asked to report whether module/unit objectives were clearly stated in each unit. While the reviewers look for solid evidencing of measurable learning objectives. One reviewer stated:

> Standard 2.2 requires that the module/ unit learning objectives describe outcomes that are measurable and consistent with the course level objectives. Many of the module level learning objectives are overlapping. It is suggested that you develop unique learning objectives for each module based on Bloom's taxonomy.

The peer reviewers had expected the course to meet this standard at or above 85% level and used this opportunity to make modification to the course toward meeting the standards.

Conclusion

Most of the items in the Online Course Evaluation Tool were designed according to the Quality Matters standards and integrate very well toward measuring the design aspect of online courses. However, the misfit items will be dropped (Item 10) or revised (Items 1, 6, 14, and 16) according to the analysis results. The results from students indicated that Tier I: *to a great extent*, Tier II: *to a moderate extent*, and Tier III: *to little or some extent*, met the standards in the three courses.

The results on most of the standards evaluated in this study provided by both reviewers and students were the same, thus indicating that both peer reviewers and students take the same point of view in terms of evidencing standards; however, they differed significantly regarding three of the essential standards. One factor possibly contributing to this discrepancy could be that reviewers looked for solid evidencing of measurable learning outcomes while students looked for clearly articulated objectives. The second factor might be that instructors clarified unclear design aspects via email while the course was delivered and not available to the reviewers. The third factor might be that the reviewers looked for above average approximately 85%, while students looked for the basic elements regarding the standards. The reviewers also perceived that the overall satisfaction of the course and the instructor might also affect students' rating regarding the essential standards. Further study, however is needed to investigate the causes of discrepancy.

References

Chickering, A., & Gamson, Z. (Eds.). (1987). Seven principles for good practice in undergraduate education. *AAHE Bulletin*, 38(7) 3-7.

Higher Learning Commission. (2007). Statement of commitment by the regional accrediting commissions for the evaluation of electronically offered degree and certificate programs. Retrieved from http://www.ncahlc.org/index.php?&Itemid=236

Holmberg, B. (1995). *Theory and practice of distance education. (2nd ed.)*. London and New York: Routledge.

Knowles, E. E., & Kalata, K. (2010, June). The impact of QM standards on learning experiences in online courses. [2009 QM Research Grant]. Presentation at the 2nd Annual Quality Matters Conference, Oak Brook, IL.

Linacre, J. M. (2009). Winsteps (Version 3.68.0) [Computer Software]. Chicago: Winsteps.com.

Quality Matters (2011). Quality Matters rubric standards 2011-2013 edition Retrieved from https://www.qmprogram.org/rubric

Ralston-Berg, P. & Nath, L. (2008). What makes a quality online course? The student perspective. 24th Annual Conference on Distance Teaching & Learning. Retrieved from http://www.uwex.edu/disted/conference/Resource_library/proceedings/08_12876.pdf

Ralston-Berg, P. (2011). What makes a quality online course? The student perspective. Presentation at the 3rd Annual Quality Matters Conference, Baltimore, MD.

Rosner, B. and Grove, D. (1999). Use of the Mann Whitney U-Test for clustered data. *Statistics*. Med. 18, 1387-1400.

Shattuck, K. (2012). *What we're learning from Quality Matters-focused research: Research, practice, continuous improvement.* Retrieved from https://www.qmprogram.org/files/Learning%20from%20QM%20Focused%20Research%20Paper_0.pdf

Shattuck, K. (2007). Quality matters: Collaborative program planning at a state level. *Online Journal of Distance Learning Administration*. Retrieved from http://www.westga.edu/~distance/ojdla/fall103/shattuck103.htm

The Higher Education Program and Policy Council (2000). *Distance education: Guidelines for good practice.* Retrieved from http://www.aft.org/pubs-reports/highered/distance.pdf

Acknowledgement

This study was sponsored by a Quality Matters research grant for 2013.

Online Course Design Evaluation Tool

The course evaluation focuses on the design of this online course, NOT the performance of your instructor. Please use the scale from 1 (To little or no extent) to 5 (To a very great extent) to make your evaluation. If an item is not applicable, leave the response blank. Thanks.

1. The purpose and structure of the course were introduced to the students.
   a. To little or no extent
   b. To some extent
   c. To a moderate extent
   d. To a great extent
   e. To a very great extent

2. The introductions of the course made clear how to get started and where find course components.
   a. To little or no extent
   b. To some extent
   c. To a moderate extent
   d. To a great extent
   e. To a very great extent

3. The communication policy and preferred form of communication were clearly stated.
   a. To little or no extent
   b. To some extent
   c. To a moderate extent
   d. To a great extent
   e. To a very great extent

4. Course objectives were clearly presented in the course syllabus.
   a. To little or no extent
   b. To some extent
   c. To a moderate extent
   d. To a great extent
   e. To a very great extent

5. Learning objectives were clearly stated for each unit or module.
   a. To little or no extent
   b. To some extent
   c. To a moderate extent
   d. To a great extent
   e. To a very great extent

6. Instructions were clearly given as to how students would meet learning objectives.
   a. To little or no extent
   b. To some extent
   c. To a moderate extent
   d. To a great extent
   e. To a very great extent

7. Instructions were clearly given as to how students would be assessed such as a detailed grading rubric for assignments.
   a. To little or no extent
   b. To some extent
   c. To a moderate extent
   d. To a great extent
   e. To a very great extent

8. The course materials were helpful for me to achieve the learning objectives.
   a. To little or no extent
   b. To some extent
   c. To a moderate extent
   d. To a great extent
   e. To a very great extent

9. The visual presentations of this course were helpful for me to achieve the learning objectives.
   a. To little or no extent
   b. To some extent
   c. To a moderate extent
   d. To a great extent
   e. To a very great extent

10. The audio or video clips in this course were helpful for me to achieve the learning objectives.
    a. To little or no extent
    b. To some extent
    c. To a moderate extent
    d. To a great extent
    e. To a very great extent

11. The resources provided in this course were relevant and useful.
    a. To little or no extent
    b. To some extent
    c. To a moderate extent
    d. To a great extent
    e. To a very great extent

12. Opportunities for engagement, including group discussions, collaboration projects, online meet-ups, virtual office hours or other use of collaboration tools were used in this course.
    a. To little or no extent
    b. To some extent
    c. To a moderate extent
    d. To a great extent
    e. To a very great extent

13. The interactive activities in the course were helpful for me to achieve the learning objectives.
    a. To little or no extent
    b. To some extent
    c. To a moderate extent
    d. To a great extent
    e. To a very great extent

14. The course quizzes/exams/assignments were consistent with the course objectives.
    a. To little or no extent
    b. To some extent
    c. To a moderate extent
    d. To a great extent
    e. To a very great extent

15. The course grading policy (e.g. how the grades were computed) was clearly stated.
    a. To little or no extent
    b. To some extent
    c. To a moderate extent
    d. To a great extent
    e. To a very great extent

16. A description of criteria used to evaluate students' work and participation in the course was clearly stated.
    a. To little or no extent
    b. To some extent
    c. To a moderate extent
    d. To a great extent
    e. To a very great extent

17. The course provided multiple opportunities for students to measure their own learning progress.
    a. To little or no extent
    b. To some extent
    c. To a moderate extent
    d. To a great extent
    e. To a very great extent

18. The tools selected for this course were easy to use.
    a. To little or no extent
    b. To some extent
    c. To a moderate extent
    d. To a great extent
    e. To a very great extent

19. Instructions were provided regarding how technology tools were used to achieve learning objectives.
    a. To little or no extent
    b. To some extent
    c. To a moderate extent
    d. To a great extent
    e. To a very great extent

20. The tools selected for this course support student learning.
   a. To little or no extent
   b. To some extent
   c. To a moderate extent
   d. To a great extent
   e. To a very great extent

21. Navigation throughout the online components of the courses was intuitive and consistent.
   a. To little or no extent
   b. To some extent
   c. To a moderate extent
   d. To a great extent
   e. To a very great extent

22. The course instruction articulated or linked to tech support.
   a. To little or no extent
   b. To some extent
   c. To a moderate extent
   d. To a great extent
   e. To a very great extent

23. The course instructions articulated or linked to other academic support services and resources.
   a. To little or no extent
   b. To some extent
   c. To a moderate extent
   d. To a great extent
   e. To a very great extent

24. The course provided information and guidance on how to access disabilities support services.
   a. To little or no extent
   b. To some extent
   c. To a moderate extent
   d. To a great extent
   e. To a very great extent

25. The course was accessible to assistive technologies such as screen readers (PDF, graphics available to screen readers, videos with captions etc.)
   a. To little or no extent
   b. To some extent
   c. To a moderate extent
   d. To a great extent
   e. To a very great extent

26. The course was well-organized.
   a. Poor
   b. Fair
   c. Good
   d. Excellent

27. Overall, how would you rate this course?
   a. Poor
   b. Fair
   c. Good
   d. Excellent

28. What parts of this course were most useful to you?

29. What parts of this course need improvement?

30. Please provide additional comments.

Many Shades of MOOCs

Deborah Adair[A], Susan W. Alman[B], Danielle Budzick[C], Linda M. Grisham[D], Mary E. Mancini[E], A. Sasha Thackaberry[F]

Massive Open Online Courses (MOOCs) represent an innovation in teaching and learning around which there is keen interest and much experimentation. MOOCs are being developed using different pedagogical approaches for different purposes and for different audiences. Starting with a theoretical framework to identify significant differences in basic approaches to MOOCs, this paper presents a set of four case studies of MOOCs developed and delivered in 2013 by four different institutions, community colleges as well as universities, on four different platforms with different approaches, purposes, and intended audiences. An examination of the association between the purpose and audience of these MOOCs, their design considerations, and their outcomes raises important questions for future research.

Keywords: MOOC, case study, connectivist, higher education, online teaching and learning, models, RN–BSN, developmental math, professional development, computer programming , library and information science, community college, Quality Matters

Introduction

In a startlingly short time frame, Massive Open Online Courses (MOOCs) have captured the interest and imagination of the higher education community and its many stakeholders. This interest is reflected in the extent of experimentation with an educational delivery model that has yet to develop a track record for effectiveness or efficiency in producing learning outcomes. Originating with a more focused constructivist pedagogy, the MOOCs developed over the last few years have moved from a connectivist learning experience toward a more traditional behaviorist approach. Today, there is experimentation on different MOOC models that reflect the diverse creativity of their faculty and developers. In fact, much of the experimentation with these new MOOCs is focused on what kinds of outcomes, for whom, and with what pedagogical frame these massive and open courses are best suited. MOOCs come in many shades; however, what counts is the achievement of purpose and the quality of the experience for the learner.

Regardless of approach, quality in instructional design is a critical component for a course meant to engage large (massive) numbers of learners who have not been through the typical institutional filters

[A] The Quality Matters Program
[B] San Jose State University
[C] Cuyahoga Community College
[D] Massachusetts Bay Community College
[E] The University of Texas at Arlington College of Nursing
[F] Cuyahoga Community College

that produce a student body more homogenous in their preparation for learning. In courses offered at large scale and that are open to an audience diverse in experiences, skills, abilities and disabilities, orientation to learning, and even language, it becomes especially critical to have a course designed to provide the communication and guidance to the learner that the course instructor can't otherwise offer at scale. Clarity and specificity in objectives, the communication of learner expectations, and guidance about how to get help or support become critical in a learning structure where the responsibility for completion and achieving learning outcomes rests almost solely on the learner.

To insure that the components of the course are clearly aligned with its purpose and objectives, many institutions rely on the Quality Matters RubricTM to guide development and to evaluate the quality of instructional design. <u>Quality Matters (QM)</u> has a version of its rubric developed for use with courses like MOOCs. <u>The QM Continuing and Professional Education Rubric (CPE Rubric)</u> is intended for the design and evaluation of online and blended courses – facilitated, mentored, or self-managed – that may have pass/fail, skills-based, or other completion or certification criteria but that do not carry academic credit. Courses to which it applies may be either instructor led or self-paced; either way, they must be structured and have completion criteria.

The QM CPE Rubric differs from the QM Higher Education Rubric in a number of ways that make it more appropriate for courses that do not bear academic credit. With the CPE Rubric, courses can meet standards without active instructor facilitation and without direct student-to-student contact. There are reduced expectations of institutional support but greater expectations for enriched student-to-content

interaction and requirements for clear descriptions of resources available to the continuing education student.

To date, QM has reviewed little more than a dozen MOOCs and, of these, only a few have met the CPE Rubric standards. Although the educational content of these MOOCs was very strong, it was clear that much less attention is being paid to the instructional design considerations that may be most important for such open enrollment courses offered at a scale outside of degree and credit-bearing programs. Such design considerations as effectively orienting the learner to the purpose and structure of the course and communicating resources and expectations are critical for learners who are not otherwise connected to the academic institution and have no other recourse to gain such information. The instructional design of MOOCs must be strong enough for students to be self-reliant and must be so well aligned with the purpose, objectives, and audience that students can succeed with the limited faculty interaction that has thus far defined the MOOC experience.

Because of the necessity for such strong alignment, the context of the MOOC is critical for its design. Placing MOOCs within the appropriate theoretical framework is one broad way to understand context. Explicitly identifying MOOCs by purpose and audience might be another. This paper will look at both perspectives, first laying out a theoretical framework to identify significant differences in approaches and then presenting a set of case studies to examine in detail the association between the purpose and audience of particular MOOCs, design considerations, and outcomes.

Theoretical Framework of MOOCs

MOOCs are a recent phenomenon in higher education. By widespread acknowledgment, the first MOOC was offered in 2008. The term itself was coined in Canada when Dave Cormier and Bryan Alexander used it to describe an open course with over 2,000 students that was free and took place at the University of Manitoba.

Since then, MOOCs have exploded in higher education, with first Ivy League institutions embracing and scaling up the trend, and new companies emerging to host MOOCs (Educause, 2012). But what specifically about the MOOC model is disruptive? Daniel writes "While the hype about MOOCs presaging a revolution in higher education has focused on their scale, the real revolution is that universities with scarcity at the heart of their business models are embracing openness" (Daniel, 2012, p. 1). The rush of institutions offering MOOCs will itself transform the landscape of higher education, or at the very least, help to precipitate change.

The very concept of disruptive innovation addresses this directly. "According to Christensen (1997), organizations that don't pay attention to disruptive innovation (1) maintain that their goods and services will always be needed, (2) develop sustaining improvements based on current customers, (3) don't understand the natural laws of disruptive innovation, and (4) fail to spin off an organization in direct competition with itself. These organizations risk becoming obsolete" (Thornton, 2013, p. 47). Institutions of higher education are particularly vulnerable to external influences during a time when funding is uncertain and pressures to perform come from students, citizens, and businesses alike (Lattuca & Stark, 2009). This directly addresses the discussion of "part of a more fundamental shift in universities" … which "is taking place at a time when the nature and purpose of the university as well as higher education are very much in question" (Blackmore & Kandiko, 2012, p. 128).

What will college education become as a result of MOOCs and other disruptive innovations? Will they persist at all?

Despite their relatively short history, MOOCs have already splintered into two distinct models for massive learning: cMOOCs and xMOOCs. "Their differences are so stark so distinct in pedagogy that it is confusing to designate them by the same term" (Hill, 2012, as cited in Daniel, 2012, p. 2). cMOOCs embrace a constructivist approach whereas xMOOCs embrace a more traditional, behaviorist approach to massive online learning.

cMOOCs refer to a constructivist or connectivist learning experience typified by the initial MOOCs that followed a more organic philosophy of interacting with resources and with fellow students to connect learning and construct knowledge. Wiley and Green describe them as applying "the 'open' ethos to course outcomes. In other words, students are empowered to learn what they need/want to learn, and the journey of learning is often more important than any predefined learning outcomes" (Wiley & Green, 2012, p. 88). cMOOCs often encompass four main types of activities: aggregation or curation of content, remixing of content, repurposing of content, and feed forward – the term referring to sharing the newly crafted knowledge with a variety of outward facing streams (Kop, Fournier, & Sui, 2011).

Is this type of MOOC effective at positively impacting student learning? While there currently exists no robust body of research on the effectiveness of MOOCs to say one way or another, there is related evidence to suggest that this model of massive education could be effective for student learning, when extrapolated from the perspective of a student's participation in a knowledge community. "Participation in these knowledge communities is both the process and the goal of learning in higher education" (Lattuca & Stark, 2009, loc 3785 of 8572). The authors go on to write that "Learning is thus a vehicle of socialization... and at the same time the result (or goal) of socialization" (Lattuca & Stark, 2009, loc 3785 of 8572). cMOOCs are uniquely set up for social learning. The development of a learning community "benefits both students and faculty, as it can lead toward better retention of students. In turn, course throughput rates increase (Santovec, 2004). There are different views on what route to follow to enable such a community to establish itself" (Nagel & Kotze, 2010, p. 46).

What implications does this model of MOOC have for the respective roles of teacher and learner? Blackmore addresses this challenge from a perspective wider than the debate about MOOCs, writing that "Increasingly, students are seen as the consumers of an educational service. Inadequate and unhelpful though the metaphor might be, it is a powerful one, challenging a more traditional relationship between teacher and student. The development of a network of colleagues with a shared view of the purposes of a change can be a powerful way of enabling a change" (Blackmore, 2012, p. 134). The demands of facilitating such learning requires facilitators "to adopt a multifaceted role so as to guide or influence the learners and communities to get involved and embrace social media practices" (Kop, Fournier, & Sui, 2011, p. 89). MOOCs as a model seem to be uniquely designed to challenge the traditional roles of teacher and student, instead framing the

concepts within the larger concept of learner-directed education, both inside and outside of institutions of higher education.

Research into early MOOCs suggests that participation in MOOCs is bifurcated further, into categories of participants and consumers. A small percentage of students who enroll in MOOCs actually fully participate. A separate group of students tend to participate via a "consuming" style, wherein they review resources and the work of fellow students, but are not active participants in the course (Kop, Fournier, & Sui, 2011).

cMOOCs have some identified challenges that aren't necessarily in play in xMOOCs. One way it is described is that the "lack of a coherent and centralized structure and a lack of summary around learning in the MOOCs also presented challenges for some participants, in particular the novice learners" (Kop, Fournier, & Sui, 2011, p. 86). There are also concerns about the level of support provided by the instructors as an ongoing challenge of the model. The degree to which the design of the course allows for peer-to-peer feedback to foster a higher level of cognitive presence can "contribute value beyond the knowledge base of the lecturer, irrespective of the large class size" (Nagel & Kotze, 2010, p. 50).

xMOOCs are also changing the educational landscape. Though far more similar to traditional online courses, xMOOCs attempt to scale learning with extremely large class sizes that are highly structured, but in which only minimal customized feedback is provided. Often more detailed feedback is provided on a peer-evaluation basis. Because of the sheer number of students in a given course, new roles have emerged for teacher and learner, wherein the teacher becomes a facilitator of the learning process.

xMOOCs are more representative of a behavioral approach that indicates a more traditional, codified, and structured educational experience far more similar to traditional online courses, but with instructional mechanisms to allow them to serve thousands of students (Daniel, 2012). EdX, Coursera, and Udacity all offer more traditional xMOOCs. An ever-expanding marketplace of xMOOCs include courses from a range of top-tier universities. There are currently efforts underway in several states to force universities to accept the successful completion of MOOCs for college credit as a way to accelerate the achievement of baccalaureate degrees.

Case Studies

The following section contains case studies of four MOOCs designed and delivered in 2013. Table 1 provides an overview of the four different institutions that implemented these MOOCs, on four different MOOC platforms, with different approaches, purposes, and intended audiences.

Case Study 1: San Jose State University, School of Library and Information Science

A MOOC Model for Professional Development

Background

The San Jose State University (SJSU) School of Library and Information Science (SLIS) is a recognized leader in online learning with a cutting-edge curriculum, offering students the convenience of a 100% online program, as well as the technology skills today's employers seek. SLIS has provided totally online programs since 2007, and the reputation for excellence is evidenced by the *2013 Sloan-C Quality Scorecard Effective Practice Award*, faculty expertise, student support, and the SJSU *Center for Information Research and Innovation*. The SLIS faculty were early adopters of the concept of MOOCs, and in Fall 2012, support was provided to develop and offer a professional development MOOC for a global audience. Course development progressed, and the first MOOC was offered in Fall 2013.

MOOC Development: Purpose, Audience, and Objectives

Two faculty members (*Michael Stephens* and *Kyle Jones*) were responsible for the design and delivery of the course, *Hyperlinked Library*, that explored how libraries are using emerging technologies to serve their diverse communities. They were supported by a team composed of faculty and MLIS students to work on the administrative, instructional, technical, and support elements of the MOOC and assist with elements of content development, design, and management. Students enrolled in the SLIS master's program (MLIS) earned academic credit for their work while students from other universities volunteered their time. In the first term, they were involved in research, site construction, instructional design, and learning how to interact with members of a virtual community. In the second term, the students led discussion groups and assisted with the delivery of the MOOC.

SJSU/SLIS is committed to offering quality professional development to individuals across the globe, and MOOCs provide a mechanism to engage a large audience. The content of the MOOCs includes cutting-edge topics that provide information professionals with an introduction to the material and enables them to explore

Institution	Platform	Type	Purpose/Course	Audience
Tri-C https://tric.coursesites.com/	Coursesites/Blackboard	xMOOC	Dev. Ed. Math	Multiple
UT Arlington https://learn.canvas.net/ courses/83	Canvas	xMOOC	RN–BSN Program "test drive," CE Continuing Education	Nurses, Providers
SJSU http://mooc.hyperlib. sjsu.edu/	Word Press and Buddy Press	cMOOC	Professional Development	LIS Professionals
Mass Bay BHCC	edX	xMOOC Blend	Intro. Computer Programming	CS and IT Undergraduates

Table 1. Four Approaches to MOOCs

the issues and network with others. The intended audience was reached through marketing and PR efforts as noted below.

Instructional Design

The design of this 10-week course used a combination of three types of learning theories in order to maximize the experience of the participants. The course developer, Michael Stephens, adapted concepts in connected learning, transformative learning, and connectivist learning to provide an environment for the users to be engaged in a variety of activities. The structure of the MOOC enabled the participants to access a wide range of resources, reflect on the content, create a project based on the experience, and share with others in the community. Details about the instructional design can be found here: https://mooc.hyperlib.sjsu.edu/about/instructional-design/

Technical Design

The course was built with an open source content management system, *WordPress*, and an open source plugin, *BuddyPress*, to provide a flexible platform for social interactions that supported the teaching philosophies. The design was proven successful since the instructors had used it to build learning environments for the prior six years. Additional information about the technical design is located here: https://mooc.hyperlib.sjsu.edu/about/technical-design/

Marketing

Promotion of the MOOC involved pages on the SLIS website: http://slisweb.sjsu.edu/programs/moocs. It included a MOOC program landing page and a page specific to the *Hyperlinked Library* MOOC:

http://slisweb.sjsu.edu/programs/moocs/hyperlinked-library-mooc. Also, there was a web page with information on how to register.

Several strategies were used, including news features on the SLIS website, emails to target audiences, and information shared via SLIS social media channels. The instructor also promoted the MOOC on his blog. Additionally, Community Profile stories about student assistants helping with the MOOC were posted online.

Outcomes and Next Steps

Enrollment was limited to 400, and many individuals interested in the MOOC were unable to register for the course. Those who participated in the 10-week course were placed in smaller groups for easier discussion, and they were encouraged to form additional groups based on special interests. Each person had the opportunity to earn individual badges after completing specific assignments and a master badge for the successful completion of the MOOC.

A second MOOC, *Exploring Future Technologies*, will be offered in Fall 2014 using the same model. Additional details are located on the *SLIS website*.

Case Study 2: The University of Texas at Arlington College of Nursing

MOOC2Degree Case Study

Background

With an enrollment approaching 33,500, the University of Texas at Arlington (UT Arlington) is the second largest institution in the UT System and the sixth largest in Texas. The University's College of Nursing (UTACON) is one of the largest and most successful in the country, with a 94% graduation rate and a first-time NCLEX (National Council Licensure Examination) pass rate consistently over 90% for new nurse graduates entering the nursing field. The New America Foundation, based in Washington, DC, has honored by UT Arlington as a Next Generation University, in part, for its success with online degree programs. More than 10,000 students were enrolled in online classes and degree programs in Fall 2013.

The College of Nursing began its development of high-volume, online programs in 2008 when it offered the university's first Academic Partnership degree-granting option – an RN-to-BSN completion program. Prior to the initiation of this program in 2008, the College of Nursing graduated approximately 100 RN-to-BSN completion students per year. In the 2012–2013 academic year, 1,746 students graduated from that program. This is the power of a dynamic, online program designed to be accessible and affordable.

MOOC Development: Purpose, Audience, and Objectives

After monitoring the expansion of MOOCs into higher education, in the summer of 2013, the University, the College of Nursing, and Academic Partnerships – a Dallas-based organization that assists universities to develop and offer scalable online programs – designed the university's first MOOC. The MOOC movement provided UT Arlington and its partner, Academic Partnerships, an opportunity to expand the online RN-to-BSN program through what is called a MOOC2Degree initiative. It was determined that this MOOC would be specifically designed to:

• Provide potential students with the ability to "Test Drive" UTACON's Aca-

demic Partnership RN-to-BSN program. This would ultimately lead to increased student enrollment.
• Provide a seamless process for awarding academic credit for students who complete the MOOC and enroll in the online RN-to-BSN program (this would help streamline the enrollment process for students).
• Provide continuing professional education to nurses in a key area within the healthcare field.
• Expand our brand and reputation as a leader in nursing education.
• Provide a community service by offering access to important information to nonnurse healthcare providers and the general public with the opportunity to receive a certificate of completion.

Instructional Design

This MOOC was designed specifically to achieve its articulated purposes. This started with the selection of the MOOC topic. The topic is important to practicing nurses and other healthcare professionals as well as one where there was an adequate amount of available open-access material to use for learning. The MOOC was entitled "Enhancing Patient Safety through Interprofessional Collaborative Practice" and was designed to be completed in six weeks with the seventh week open for those learners who wished to take the proctored final examination.

As the primary intent of the course was to allow students to "Test Drive" online education, no payment was required until course completion when the learner decided on his or her desired endpoint – credit toward a required course in the RN-to-BSN program or Continuing Education Units (CEU) credit. Consistent with the core belief of open access in MOOCs, the costs to the learners were "pay to play." Entrance into the MOOC was free of charge. Learners who wished to receive academic credit in UTACONs RN-to-BSN program enrolled to take a final summative examination and paid the online proctoring service directly for that service (<$30 with the fee varying dependent upon the individual's preference for when the examination was scheduled). The only additional charge for receiving credit was that associated with the established process for receiving "credit by exam" ($25). Learners, who wished to receive CEU for the course, paid the CE provider $25 for obtaining a certificate for the 45 hours of continuing education credit.

An Operations Team was responsible for identifying the flow of information to allow individuals to sign up for the MOOC, participate, and reach their desired end point (academic credit, continuing education credit, certificate of completion) in a seamless way. Individuals on this team include representatives from the university's Departments of Distance Education and Admissions along with the College of Nursing and Academic Partnerships.

A Course Development team was responsible for the content and the presentation of the course. After review, a decision was made to use Canvas Open Network as the Learning Management System. Identification of course objectives, learning outcomes, curricula flow, and included content and evaluation methods were the responsibility of the course faculty. Media experts and instructional designers from Academic Partnerships assisted in course construction on the Canvas Open Network. Working collaboratively, open access learning artifacts appropriate to the course objectives were identified so as to avoid any costs associated with books or other supplementary material.

Outcomes and Next Steps

In August 2013, the course went live with a "soft launch" – limited enrollment – to pilot test the course structure and processes. On the start date, there were approximately 300 learners enrolled. In a start of the course survey, the following information was obtained:

Country of origin

- 70% were from the United States
- 9% were from Western Europe
- 7% were from Africa
- 4% were from South America
- 2% were from Central/East Asia
- English was the primary language for 75% of the participants

Professional discipline (see Figure 1)

- 57% of respondents were nurses.
- 43% of these respondents were interested in course credit
- 14% were interested in CEUs

Figure 1. Breakdown of respondents by profession.

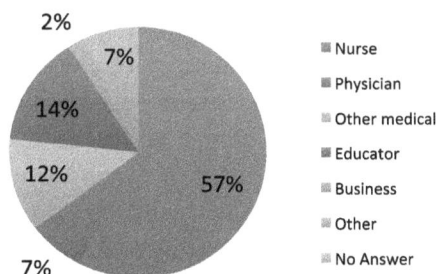

Learner experience

In later surveys, additional data were collected about learners' experience. The course load was in line with learner expectations. Learners expected between 2 and 4 hours of work a week. At mid-course, 66% thought course load was manageable. At the end of the course, 80% felt the course length was appropriate. Furthermore, 90% of the students gave the course a 4- or 5-star rating, which included comments such as:

- "I would like to have more of every-thing."
- "Great and very informative."
- "I thoroughly enjoyed this course.... It has provided me with some amazing resources to consult and dig deeper into. I am very motivated to continue to study this issue further and start seeking out opportunities to get involved in organizations focused on improving healthcare through educating others in IP collaboration."
- "The case studies give examples of real life scenarios which make me think critically. The follow up discussion opens my mind to other people's opinions."

The case studies (using Team STEPPS videos from the Agency for Healthcare Research and Quality) and discussion, "From My Perspective" videos, and the lecture videos were favorites (see Figure 2). While Twitter Chat was in the course design as an engagement strategy, there was virtually no engagement with these activities. On reflection, this is perhaps not unexpected given a target audience that includes a large number of nurses who had limited experience with online education. The other interactive activities were found to be very engaging.

Figure 2. Favorite part of the course.

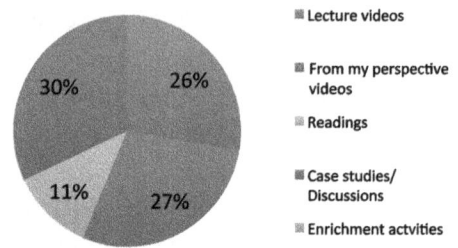

- Lecture videos
- From my perspective videos
- Readings
- Case studies/ Discussions
- Enrichment actvities

Course completion

An interesting challenge appeared when new learners continued to enroll in the course up through the last week. This was challenging, as the group had built engagement activities into the course with the assumption that the active cohort of learners would stay reasonably constant. How best to design the MOOC to deal with new learners who join while the course is in session is something the group will be addressing in future iterations of the course.

Understanding completion rates is one of the major challenges with MOOCs and UTACON is currently considering what approach to take when reporting completion rates. For example, should one measure success by using the total number of individuals who enroll at any point in the MOOC as the denominator, only the ones who had some level of instructional activity, or only those who expressed in an interest in achieving the goals for the course? There is much debate in the literature right now about this issue. Based on our experience, there is a critical need for more robust subgroup analysis so as to understand how to define and quantify success.

Of twenty-nine registered nurses who responded to a participant survey within the MOOC, twenty-eight expressed interest in applying to UTACON's RN-to-BSN program and receiving academic credit. By the time the MOOC closed, 50% of these were already moving forward with the application process.

Lessons learned

There were numerous lessons learned as part of this offering. Developing a MOOC is different than developing a traditional course as the learners have different motivations; course developers need to be clear about what they want to accomplish for the course and build with the learner's goals in mind. It is also important to focus on engagement strategies and develop a sense of community ("high touch") even though you are constructing the course to be "low touch" from the perspective of faculty/facilitators. For discussions, it is helpful to use case studies revolving around actual patient care situations and use facilitators to help students feel more engaged with the course and the instructor. It is also important to determine if the course will run in a set "term" or run "open access." Obtaining useful metrics is difficult – but critical – and needs to be considered from the start. Developing an evaluation plan should not be an after-thought. It is important to have a clear definition of "success" and a plan to assess for any mid-course corrections or revisions when running the course again is critical.

UTACON's inaugural MOOC2Degree effort provided important information that will inform the approach taken in the future with the initiative. In particular, it provided valuable insight into the ways that MOOCs differ from traditional for-credit courses and the ways in which the group might consider adapting our approach as it relates to course design, student engagement, and measurement in the future. Early indicators give the group reason to

be enthusiastic about the potential of this initiative, and this group looks forward to sharing more detailed results once it has implemented the initiative on a broader scale.

Case Study 3: Cuyahoga Community College, Development Mathematics MOOC

A Competency-Driven MOOC Using Game-Based Mechanics

Background

Cuyahoga Community College (Tri-C) is a multicampus college in Cleveland, Ohio, serving over 52,000 credit and noncredit students. As an Achieving the Dream Leader College, Tri-C has committed substantial staff and financial resources to develop, implement, and evaluate highly structured, multiyear initiatives designed to improve student success. The College is a member of the League for Innovation in the Community College, a 19-member international organization committed to improving community colleges through innovation, experimentation, and institutional transformation. In Fall 2013, Tri-C was awarded one of the Bill & Melinda Gates Foundation grants to expedite the transition into mainstream college coursework for massive numbers of development education students. This was the beginning of turning the vision into a reality.

The Tri-C MOOC ran four separate offerings: March, April, May, and June 2013. These were four faculty-facilitated offerings each spanning four weeks. The Tri-C faculty also utilized the MOOC content in one blended offering during Summer 2013.

MOOC Development: Purpose, Audience, and Objectives

The goal of designing and developing a Developmental Mathematics MOOC was to leverage the college's extensive experience in subject matter and online learning to expedite the transition into mainstream college coursework for massive numbers of students.

In the Fall 2011 semester, Tri-C had 2,285 "new-to-college" students test into the College's first-level developmental mathematics course – MATH 0910 – Basic Arithmetic and Pre-Algebra. In the Spring 2012 semester, another 1,109 students tested into this course. Of these, nearly 3,400 students, approximately 1,600 tested at the upper end of the placement score range for the MATH 0910 course. Tri-C's Developmental Mathematics MOOC targeted these students who tested into the upper levels of pre-algebra. The MOOC was intended to bridge the gap for these students, allowing them to skip the college's MATH 0910 course altogether and go directly into the college's Beginning Algebra or Quantway course sequence. The overarching outcomes for the MOOC pilot included:

• Addressing the developmental education challenge and Tri -C's priority to help students get to college ready status at a faster pace.
• Opportunities for partnership with K-12 by targeting high schools students and helping students get to college-ready status before they enroll at Tri-C.
• Supporting returning students who want/need a brief math refresher.
• Contributing to the exploration of innovative and experiential practices in teaching and learning and being a leader among community colleges, as a Board Member Institution in the League for Innovation in the Community College.

The audience for the MOOC included a number of different student populations – both current students and nonstudents. These audiences included students currently enrolled in Tri-C's bridge courses, as well as students who desired additional practice after completing mandatory placement prep. Tri-C's work with local high school partnerships and the community also expanded the target audience to first generation, returning, post-secondary, and tech-prep students. Lastly, in partnership with Blackboard Coursesites, Tri-C was able to enroll students outside the region, state, and nation.

Instructional Design

The Tri-C Math MOOC was developed by a collaborative team of faculty and instructional designers. Several faculty members served as subject matter experts and members of the instructional design team served as both designers and developers, supporting the faculty by aligning the course, developing the course structure in the Learning Management System, loading the vetted content and materials, and setting up adaptive release for the gaming aspect of the learning experience. Finally, an external graphics developer provided unique graphics for the entire course.

The course was designed and developed during a two-month period (January–February 2013), as the first offering was scheduled for March 2013. This required a high level of interaction between the faculty and the design team, needing regular communication, quick turnaround times, and collaboration. The collaboration was critical to the success of the project, and working together, the full team was able to fix technical issues, adapt the course as needed, and improve the support to students.

Game mechanics

The MOOC was designed using game mechanics with a storyline (similar to the reality television show "Survivor") about the world of math challenges on "Believe Island." The course consisted of four different levels for the competencies related to Tri-C's lowest level of developmental math. In each level, students were able to interact with a variety of open educational resources, including an open educational textbook, instructional videos, and practice activities. Once they felt confident, students were then required to complete both checkpoints and challenges. Each checkpoint helped the students as a "self-test" on their proficiency of a key concept, while the challenges were designed to demonstrate mastery of all the concepts in a particular level. Students had to complete the challenge with a score of 80% or better. If they successfully completed, students "leveled up" into the next level of the course and earned a virtual badge (integrated with Mozilla Open Badges). If students did not earn an 80%, they had the opportunity to complete the challenge as many times as they needed based on a random block question pool developed by the faculty subject matter experts. The challenges created a low-risk, safe-failure environment to encourage persistence in the learners.

Open educational resources

The Tri-C MOOC did not recreate the wheel. Instead, the course was designed using existing open learning objects for the Pre-Algebra MOOC. This included the open textbook, videos, practice activities, and more. The checkpoint and the challenge questions were developed by the faculty.

The selection and vetting process to align the OER with the course objectives was a time-consuming task. The faculty worked collaboratively with the instructional designers to vet and view the resources through Kahn Academy, Connexions, Teacher Tube, and other sources. Tri-C also openly licensed, through Creative Commons, the images and the entire course for use by any nonprofit institution.

Quality Matters

Tri-C's Developmental Math MOOC was designed with the principles of QM in mind. The course site was the first MOOC in the country to earn QM recognition via the QM CPE Rubric (Quality Matters, 2014). This demonstrates that MOOCs can indeed meet high standard of course design quality. *Course video tour.*

An overview of the full course design can be found in the navigational video at http://www.youtube.com/embed/kMeh-DOaVtHo.

Technical Design

The course was designed in *Blackboard Course* sites, using open educational resources from Khan Academy and a number of additional repositories. Students could register and enroll directly in the Blackboard Course sites to gain access to the course.

Marketing

Tri-C used a number of different marketing strategies to reach out to the multiple audiences, including: (1) informational flyers – (in both print and virtual formats), (2) emails, (3) webpages – Tri-C's website and the eLearning & Innovation blog, (4) face-to-face communication at the testing centers where students complete the placement tests, and (5) collaboration with a number of local high schools. Furthermore, the Ohio Board of Regents and the Ohio Association of Community College shared the MOOC information via listserv to the state-wide memberships.

Outcomes and Next Steps

The process of designing, developing, and implementing Tri-C's MOOC was a definite success with a number of learning opportunities for best practices. The collaborative and iterative design and development process, partnering a team of faculty with instructional designers, worked extremely well to deliver the MOOC in a short time frame.

Figure 3 provides an overview of the total number of students engaged at each level. The total success and completion rate equaled 18.4%, which is nearly double the national average. The results indicate that the incorporation of low-tech game mechanics in the course through the use of adaptive release may

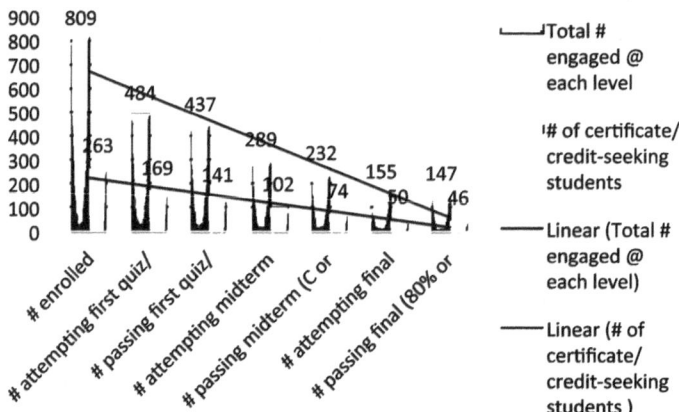

Figure 3. Total number of students engaged at each level versus number of certificate/credit seeking students engaged at each level.

have been one of the reasons for success. The low-risk, low-failure learning created by the game-based learning strategies proved successful for this MOOC for a developmental education audience and may prove beneficial for all MOOCs.

Gates grant report results

•The full MOOC Report can be found at https://breeze.tri-c.edu/moocreport/, which includes MOOC completion rates

by age group and satisfaction data.
•Keep up on the latest about Tri-C's MOOCs at http://elearningandinnova-tion.com/pilots-and-initiatives/moocs/.

Case Study 4: Massachusetts Bay Community College and Bunker Hill Community College

xMOOC Content Implementation: Community College MIT edX Partnership

Background

The edX organization at MIT, Massachusetts Institute of Technology, Cambridge, MA ("edX Home Page," 2014) approached Massachusetts Bay Community College (MassBay) in August 2012 and proposed that Mass-Bay offer the MITx MOOC course, 6.00x *Introduction to Computer Science and Programming* to MassBay students in a blended (hybrid) format ("edX Intro Python," 2013).

The community college instructor would use (in whole or part) the MITX 6.00x MOOC course content (syllabus, course materials, video lectures, problem sets, exams, etc.) in a pilot course in spring semester 2013. Bunker Hill Community College (BHCC) was invited in September 2012 to participate in the project.

MassBay, located in Wellesley Hills, and BHCC, located in Boston, are both multicampus, urban institutions in the greater Boston area with many students from low-income and underrepresented communities. MassBay and BHCC serve 6,500 and 14,000 full and part-time students, respectively. Both schools are comprehensive colleges; MassBay and BHCC offer 70+ and 100+ associate and certificate degree programs, respectively. BHCC serves a highly diverse student population with 67% students of color ("BHCC Fast Facts," 2014). MassBay similarly serves a diverse student body where 44% are students of color ("MassBay Fast Facts," 2014).

MassBay's Computer Science Department has a larger computer science associate's degree program in comparison to BHCC's Information Technology Department which offers large computer support, database, networking, and computer security degree programs, along with a small computer science program. Instructors at both colleges were identified to develop courses to implement the MITx 6.00x course for blended (hybrid) delivery in spring semester 2013.

MOOC Development: Purpose, Audience, and Objectives

This edX-Community College Partnership, funded by the Bill and Melinda Gate Foundation, was established to conduct the first empirical study exploring the efficacy of offering massive open online courses (MOOCs) for college course credit in a more traditional community college setting (Bell, Hunter, L'heureux, and Petersen, 2013).

Important Project Research Questions:

- Can community colleges (and other credit granting institutions) adopt and use MOOCs to benefit their students?

- To what extent do edX courses (and MOOCs in general) need modification for delivery in a community college classroom?
- How do different types of students respond to the flipped classroom approach?
- How does the community college student experiences (and performance) compare to those students who have completed the same course as a MOOC in the Fall 2012?
- What support does the faculty need to use the edX courseware? How are institutions able to support them?
- Is this a scalable approach for community college courses in computer science?

This project focused on two audiences: (a) U.S. community colleges and (b) the highly diverse (i.e., by income, gender, age, race, ethnicity, language, prior academic preparation, especially in mathematics) undergraduate student populations commonly served by community colleges.

The edX MOOC course, 6.00x *Introduction to Computer Science and Programming Using Python*, is similar in content and structure to a course taken by noncomputer science majors at MIT. 6.00x was "designed to help people with no prior exposure to computer science or programming learning to think computationally and write programs to tackle useful problems" ("edX Intro Python," 2013). The MIT edX 6.00x MOOC ran for the first time in fall 2012 with roughly 20,000 participants active in the MOOC (over 80,000 had enrolled initially).

During the fall 2012 semester, a team of faculty at MassBay and members of the BHCC's Computer Information Technology Department worked with edX administrators and technical staff to design distinctly different courses in order to address differences in students' math proficiency at the two colleges. The majority of the MassBay students were computer science majors. However, these blended courses both used the MITx 6.00x MOOC course unchanged (including the problem sets and exams). The MassBay course, CS 270 *Practical Python Programming*, followed the same schedule as the MITx 6.00x MOOC course. The BHCC course CIT *Python Programming*, would progress more slowly through the MITx 6.00x MOOC materials – completing seven of the original 14 weeks (Bell, Hunter, L'heureux, and Petersen, 2013; "MCO-Keynote," 2013).

The MITx 6.00x MOOC course was analyzed with regard to its organization, pedagogical style, course outcomes, video lectures, activities, support materials, etc. The instructors at both community colleges recognized that the in-class sessions needed to give students a holistic and clear understanding of the academic challenges to be addressed in the MITx 6.00x MOOC assignments. The community college instructors supplied the missing "alignments" or "scaffolding" between MITx 6.00x MOOC course outcomes and the individual MITx 6.00x MOOC assignments.

Discussions during the course design phase on how best to support students given the differences in the math comfort levels and prior programming experiences between MassBay and BHCC students led to different pedagogical approaches. Only 29% of BHCC students had taken at least one college programming course, compared to 83% of MassBay students (Bell, Hunter, L'heureux, and Petersen, 2013).

The MassBay instructor adapted course materials used to teach a previous programming course and created online "notebooks." These short tutorials, that MassBay students accessed online, contained supplemental materials and interactive preparatory exercises so that students could independently complete their MITx 6.00x MOOC assignments and tests. At the weekly classroom sessions, the MassBay instructor primarily worked, as needed, with students singularly or in small groups; lectures were rare. The MassBay course, CS 270 *Practical Python Programming*, followed the same timetable and schedule as the MITx 6.00x MOOC course.

The BHCC instructors elected to teach more traditionally with lectures and small group work with many hands-on activities. Student met twice weekly with their instructors. The BHCC course, CIT 523 *Python Programming*, used the same content but at a slower pace, such that seven weeks of the MITx 6.000x MOOC materials were covered by the end of the Spring 2013 semester rather than the full 14 weeks. BHCC students could still access the remainder of the course materials and finish the MITx 6.00x MOOC course on their own so they might qualify for the edX completion certificate.

Instructional Design

MassBay and BHCC courses were designed to support the "flipped classroom" pedagogy. Students accessed MITx 6.000x MOOC materials online: watched the online videos; performed the online exercises; submitted the online homework; and took the online tests (the edX platform supported instant scoring, feedback, and multiple submission attempts) just like any MITx 6.00x MOOC student. Students at each community college had required classroom meetings each week. At MassBay, students met for one 90-minute session; BHCC students met twice weekly for 60-minute sessions. The community college students participated in classroom activities, completed additional homework assignments, and took in-class exams.

Technical Design

The community college courses were mounted on the stand-alone edX LMS platform developed by edX during Fall 2012 and piloted for this project. The entire MITx 6.00x course was copied into what has become the "Open edX" platform ("Open edX code," 2014). MassBay and BHCC instructors could independently access their respective course shells to insert announcements, set up discussion forums, etc. The edX staff provided extensive technical support throughout the design phase and during the Spring 2013 semester.

Implementation

The pilot courses (CS 270 and CTI 523) ran once, starting in January and ending in May, 2013. Students registered for these college credit-bearing (and transferable) courses at their respective colleges, as usual. Upon completion of the course, students received a final (letter) grade along with the opportunity to qualify for the certificate of completion issued by edX. A student thus could be successful in the course by completing the stated course requirements in the syllabus for CS 270 or CIT 523 and not qualify for the edX certificate.

Marketing

MassBay and BHCC recruited students internally through informational flyers, posters, emails, and a specially produced edX video posted on the websites ("edX-BHCC," 2013; "edX-MassBay," 2013). However, the most effective approach was to visit classrooms in fall 2012 and explain the project with its potential benefits to the students.

Outcomes and Next Steps

Dr. Damien Bell, the edX evaluator from Boston College, conducted interviews, and completed pre- and postsurveys of students' and instructors' perspectives at both colleges. He conducted student focus groups, gathered data on student participation for in-class and online course activities, and made classroom observations (Bell, Hunter, L'heureux, and Petersen, 2013). Preliminary analysis of project results demonstrates that students at both community colleges were able to handle the MITx 6.00x MOOC course materials with structured, in-class support from their instructors. The MassBay and BHCC students' overall academic performance was better than that of the participants in the Fall 2012 MITx 6.00x MOOC where the great majority of those that earned the MITx completion certificates had at least a bachelor's degree or higher. The Fall 2012 MITx 6.00x MOOC started with around 20,000 active students. Of the roughly 11,000 who took the MITx 6.00x MOOC midterm exam, 59% passed compared to 90% of the community college students that tested (N= 29). The retention rate was better for the community college students. Of the original 40 community college students (21 at MassBay; 10 at BHCC), 73% took the MITx 6.00x midterm exam and 26 students (65%) completed their courses (and also earned MITx completion certificates). For the Fall 2012 MITx 6.00x MOOC, about 5,000 participants (~25% of the original 20,000) successfully finished the course and earned the MITx completion certificate (Bell, Hunter, L'heureux, and Petersen, 2013; "MCO-Keynote," 2013). The final report with the full analysis of this project is expected in Spring 2014.

Discussion and Conclusion

The four case studies highlight the kind of experimentation on MOOCs occurring in higher education today. As the purpose and audience for MOOCs vary, so do their design and development. Each of the MOOCs described here was a learning experience for its institution and its individuals – developers, instructors, and students alike. MOOCs will continue to evolve as we continue to experiment, examine the outcomes, and continually improve our efforts as a result. As is the case in the most effective experimentation, the questions being raised by these MOOCs and others are often the most important part of the innovation.

These MOOCs were designed for a variety of different audiences; however, can every kind of learner take advantage of MOOCs? What adaptations need to be made – in pedagogy, design, or content – to accommodate those learners who would otherwise be disadvantaged by a MOOC approach?

Do low completion rates of MOOCs matter? What other success measures, in addition to or instead of completion, are important? Will the integration of game mechanics or related techniques improve engagement and completion? Does a blended learning structure improve performance and completion rates?

Should MOOCs offer college credit and/or should learners receive credit after-the-fact for MOOCs? What criteria need to be met for MOOCs to be credit-worthy? Can a single MOOC support multiple purposes or outcomes; in particular, can it effectively provide multiple completion pathways to include credit toward degree? Can it be an important piece of such a pathway?

Is grading at scale possible? With the appropriate software, can machine grading be effective in all courses? How can automated grading software be used to promote student engagement?

With MOOCs, one of the biggest attractions is also the biggest challenge. MOOCs provide a learning platform that can bring together hundreds to hundreds of thousands of learners in a single course. Sharing the platform, however, is much different and far simpler than engaging in shared learning. The creation of real learning communities is made more challenging by scale, not easier, in the behaviorist approach of the xMOOC. Yet, such communities and the learning they afford may be essential to the awarding of academic credit in all but direct assessment models. This challenge is one reason the next generation of MOOC experimentation involves blended learning models where the learning community is nurtured outside of the MOOC and the MOOC becomes the high-quality material with which the community engages. In these models, MOOCs are transitioning from online course to online content.

It is still very early in the development of the MOOC model to fully understand the potential of MOOCs and the lessons we can learn from them about teaching with technology. Whether their future is as scalable online courses, content supplements, or something altogether different, the energy and momentum they have created for experimentation around teaching and learning is a singular achievement. Regardless of the shade of any particular MOOC, their lasting impact will be to energize the field to understand, improve, and enhance the quality of the educational experience for the learner.

References

Blackmore, P., & Kandiko, C. (2012). *Strategic curriculum change: Global trends in universities*. Milton Park, Abingdon: Routledge.

Bell, D., Hunter, L., L'heureux, J., & Petersen, R. (2013). *MOOCs in the Community College: Implications for innovation in the classroom*. Retrieved from http://sloan-consortium.org/conference/2013/blended/moocs-community-college-implications-innovation-classroom

Bunker Hill Community College – Fast Facts. (2014) Retrieved from http://www.bhcc.mass.edu/about/institutionaleffectiveness/fastfacts/

Educause (2012). *What campus leaders need to know about MOOCs*. Retrieved from http://net.educause.edu/ir/library/pdf/PUB4005.pdf

Daniel, J. (2012). *Making Sense of MOOCs: Musings in a Maze of Myth, Paradox and Possibility*. Retrieved from Academic Partnerships website: http://www.academicpartnerships.com/research/white-paper-making-sense-of-moocs.

edX Bunker Hill Community College student recruitment. (2013). Retrieved from http://www.bhcc.mass.edu/edx/

edX Home Page. (2014). Retrieved January 14, 2014, from https://www.edx.org/

edX Introduction to Computer Science and Programming Python. (2013). Retrieved January 14, 2014, from https://www.edx.org/course/mitx/mitx-6-00-1x-introduction-computer-1122

edX Massachusetts Bay Community College student recruitment. (2013). Retrieved from http://www.massbay.edu/Academics/New-Course--Practical-Python-Programming.aspx

Kop, R., Fournier, H., & Mak, J. (2011). A pedagogy of abundance or a pedagogy to support human beings? Participant support on massive open online courses. *International Review of Research in Open and Distance Learning*, 12(7), 74–93.

Lattuca, L. R., & Stark, J. S. (2009). *Shaping the college curriculum: Academic plans in context* (2nd ed.). San Francisco, CA: Jossey-Bass.

Massachusetts Colleges Online Conference – Keynote Address by O'Donnell, P., R., Bell, D., & L., L'heureux, J. (2013). *MOOCs on campus: A closer examination*. Retrieved from http://www.mco.mass.edu/conference/

Nagel, L., & Kotze, T. G. (2010). Supersizing e-learning: What a CoI survey reveals about teaching presence in a large online class. *Internet and Higher Education*, 13(1–2), 45–51.

Open edX source code. (2014). Retrieved from http://code.edx.org/

Quality Matters (2014). *Quality Matters continuing and professional education rubric*. Retrieved from https://www.quality-matters.org/continuing-and-professional-education-rubric-program

Thornton, J. S. (2013). Community colleges: Ready to disrupt again. In R. Glaspar & G. E. De los Santos (Eds.), *Disruptive innovation and the community college* (pp. 41–49). Retrieved from http://league.org/publica-

tion/whitepapers/files/Disruptive Innovation and the Community College.pdf

Wiley, D., & Green, C. (2012). Why openness in education? In *Game changers: Education andinformation technologies* (6).
Retrieved from http://www.educause.edu/
research-publications/books/game-chang-
ers-education-and-information-technolo-
gies

Effect of Student Readiness on Student Success in Online Courses

Leah A. Geiger[A], Daphne Morris[B], Susan L. Suboez[C], Kay Shattuck[D], Arthur Viterito[E]

This research determined the effect of student readiness on student success in online courses that were of quality course design; were taught by experienced, engaging instructors; and were delivered within a well-supported and familiar Learning Management System (LMS). The research team hypothesized that student success in well-designed courses (those that meet the Quality Matters standards) and that are taught by experienced, engaging faculty is most influenced by student readiness factors, including individual attributes (such as motivation), life factors, comprehension, general knowledge, reading rate and recall, and typing speed and accuracy. A goal of the study was to determine which of these factors correlated most closely to student success. Results of this study indicated that, when course design, instruction, and LMS are held constant, only typing speed/accuracy and reading rate/recall were statistically significant as measured by the SmarterMeasure instrument and correlated to student course retention and course grade. Recommendations for further research are made.

Keywords: student readiness, course design, course retention, student success, online instructors

Student success in online learning continues to rightfully receive a lot of research and practice attention. That success has been measured by student satisfaction (Allen, Omori, Burrell, Mabry, & Timmerman, 2013; Aman, 2009), by levels of engagement (Hall, 2010), by grades (Swan, Matthews, & Bogle, 2010; Swan, Matthews, Bogle, Boles, & Day, 2011; Runyon, 2006), and by course persistence (Sherrill, 2012; Harkness, Soodjinda, Hamilton, & Bolig, 2011; Pittenger & Doering, 2010; Diaz & Cartnal, 2006; Dietz-Uhler, Fisher, & Han, 2007) and program reten-

tion (Boston, Ice, & Gibson, 2011). It is a complicated process to identify the correlations among the factors that influence student success. The impact of student characteristics (Moore & Kearsley, 2012; Jung, 2012; Poellhuber, Roy, & Anderson, 2011; Hall, 2011; Battalio, 2009; Wojciechowski & Palmer, 2005), of online learning experience (Adkins, 2013; Sherrill, 2012; Boston, Ice, & Burgess, 2012), of the design of a course (Naidu, 2013), of institutionally provided academic, counseling (Curry, 2013), and technical supports (Jung, 2012), of the skills and engagement of the

---

[A] College of Southern Maryland
[B] College of Southern Maryland
[C] College of Southern Maryland
[D] Director of Research, Quality Matters Program
[E] College of Southern Maryland

instructor (Stavredes & Herder, 2013; Jung & Latchem, 2012; Swan, 2012; Rutland & Diomede, 2011), and of familiarity with technology have been identified as impacting the success of online student learning.

This research project stemmed from a recommendation coming out of a study conducted by Jurgen Hilke (2010) for Maryland Online. He inquired as to why students withdraw from online classes. Four clusters of related factors were identified as obstacles for students completing an online course: (1) student chooses too many courses; (2) student gets behind in the course; (3) student experiences personal and family-related problems; and (4) student cannot cope with the combined workload of employment and academic studies (p. 7). As a result of these findings, he recommended further investigation into "an analysis of variables for inclusion into a potential regression model to predict online course retention" (p. 9). Student orientation to distance learning was one of the areas of possible intervention recommended. This research was inspired by Hilke's call for a further analysis of intervening variables.

The College of Southern Maryland (CSM) is a regionally accredited community college located in the mid-Atlantic, serving three counties of mixed social and economic demographics. CSM was one of the Maryland community colleges, that in 2002, field-tested what would become the Quality Matters Rubric™ and process for the continuous improvement of online learning. CSM is committed to strengthening quality assurance for students, faculty, and community with specific focus on continuing to design and to have all CSM online courses meet Quality Matters (QM) standards.

The SmarterMeasure™ student readiness assessment was identified as a vetted instrument to provide analysis of a number of variables identified in the Hilke study that might impact success in online courses. SmarterMeasure Learning Readiness indicator is a web-based tool to access a learner's likelihood for succeeding in an online and/or technology-rich learning program (para. 1). Previously, Argosy University had conducted research using SmarterMeasure and found "statistically significant relationships of technical competency, motivations, availability of time, and retention" (SmarterMeasures, Research Results, para. 4). The CSM study originated as a replication and extension of the Argosy study by collecting data from courses that meet QM standards (defined as a well-designed online course), and that were taught by experienced online instructors with established positive track records of student engagement and who were highly trained in the LMS and instructional design. The rationale for including these inputs to quality online learning was to hold constant three known influencing factors in student success: course design, instructor engagement, and familiarity and support of technology (LMS). The intent of this research was to determine the effect of student readiness on student success in online courses. The aim of this research project was to offer direction for student remediation in order to better prepare students for online learning and enhance student success, while noting the possible impact of course design and engaging instructor recommendations to enhance the quality of online learning.

Methodology

The study was conducted over two semesters. The disciplines of the courses varied (Fundamentals of Physics, Introduction to Sociology, and Applied Business Communications), but were first-year college courses. All three instructors had over seven years of online teaching experience each teaching online and had established student engagement skills. Additionally, all three had successfully completed at least two QM professional development trainings, were certified QM Master Reviewers, and had been active participants in the Middle States accreditation process.

Participants

The data collected in this study occurred in 11 classes with a total of 200 students over the period of two semesters – Fall 2012 and Spring 2013. Students were required to take the SmarterMeasure Learning Readiness Indicator before beginning the course work. The Indicator is a vetted web-based tool which assesses a learner's likelihood for succeeding in an online and/or technology-rich learning program by measuring the degree to which an individual student possesses attributes, skills, and knowledge that contribute to success. At the end of the semester, a correlational analysis was run to measure the relationships between SmarterMeasure scores and measures of course retention and grade distribution as measures of academic success. The study was conducted for two semesters to ensure a valid data pool.

SmarterMeasure data for six indicators were aggregated based on a percentage scale of 0% to 100%. The six indicators include On-screen Reading Rate and Recall; Typing Speed and Accuracy; Life Factors; Technical Knowledge; Reading Comprehension; and Individual Attributes (including motivation, procrastination, and willingness to ask for help). The final grades earned for the selected CSM courses was aggregated and rated by academic success. The findings were analyzed through Chi square tests for statistical significance. At the

end of the semesters, we conducted a statistical analysis to measure the relationships between SmarterMeasure scores and CSM measures of course retention and grade distribution as measures of academic success.

Statistical Analysis

A Chi squared analysis was conducted to search for statistical significance to the scores of the SmarterMeasure assessment compared to the final course grades the students earned in the selected course sections. The six SmarterMeasure indicators scores were aggregated and compared to the final grade the individual student earned in the course. SmarterMeasure scores rely on student answers, some being subjective (life factors and individual attributes) as well as objective measures.

The scores from the SmarterMeasure assessment are delivered as ranges being labeled blue for rates between 85% and 100%; labeled green for rates between 70% and 84%; and labeled red for rates between 0% and 69%. As we analyzed the data, we realized that (a) there were a number of small cells, and (c) there were "zero" cells. Therefore, as per acceptable social statistical analysis, the only practical alternative was to combine categories in such a manner as to eliminate these small and zero cells. The red cells were highly problematic in most of the cases; therefore, we combined the green and red labels (frequencies) to eliminate any biasing that the low red frequencies may have introduced into the analysis. Therefore, we used two SmarterMeasure Indicator Rates – (a) students earning a rate from 85% to 100% (the blue labels), and (b) students earning a rate from 0% to 84% (the green and red labels, combined).

The final grades for the class were measured as "successful" at the rate of 70%

or higher, equating to a letter grade of C, B, or A. CSM policy supports this valuation, as 70% is the cut-off score for credit being earned for the course as well as its ability to be transferred to another school. In addition, the majority of student learning outcomes assessments at CSM use the benchmark of 70% or higher.

Results

At the 95% confidence level, two of the SmarterMeasure indicators (typing speed/accuracy and reading rate/recall) were statistically significant, thereby exerting significant influence on student success in the course. There is a high probability (at the 95% level) that the other SmarterMeasure indicators did not exert significant influence on student success. See Table 1 for the aggregate data.

SmarterMeasure Indicator, Reading Rate

The results for reading rate and recall indicate with a high degree of confidence that this indicator exerts an influence on student success. Specifically, 72 students were successful per the SmarterMeasure Indicator, while 62 ended up being successful in the course. The results are statistically significant, α = .05. See Figure 1.

SmarterMeasure Indicator, Typing Speed

The results for typing speed and accuracy indicate with a high degree of confidence that this indicator exerts an influence on student success. Specifically, 88 students were successful per the SmarterMeasure Indicator, while 81 ended up being successful in the course. The results are statistically significant, α = .05. See Figure 2.

SmarterMeasure Indicator, Life Factors

The results for life factors do not show that this indicator exerts an influence on student success. The results are not statistically significant, α = .05. (Note that there is a statistical significance only if you set the alpha at the .1 level.) See Figure 3.

SmarterMeasure Indicator, Technical Knowledge

The results for technical knowledge do not show that this indicator exerts an influence on student success. The results are not statistically significant, α = .05. (Note that there is a statistical significance only if you set the alpha at the .1 level). See Figure 4.

SmarterMeasure Indicator, Reading Comprehension

The results for technical knowledge do not show that this indicator exerts a significant influence on student success, as the results are not statistically significant, α = .05. See Figure 5.

SmarterMeasure Indicator, Individual Attributes

The results for individual attributes do not show that this indicator exerts an influence on student success. The results are not statistically significant, α = .05. See Figure 6.

Discussion

The study was based on the hypothesis that student success in well-designed courses (those that meet QM standards), that are delivered via a familiar LMS, and that are taught by experienced and engaging online instructors are most influenced

Table 1. SmarterMeasure Indicators Compared to Final

Indicator Name	Final Grade Earned	Indicator Rate at 85% to 100%	Indicator Rate at 0% to 84%	Total (N)
Reading Rate*	Successful	62	12	74
	Not Successful	10	6	16
	Total	72	18	90
Typing Speed*	Successful	81	59	140
	Not Successful	7	14	21
	Total	88	73	161
Life Factors	Successful	49	122	171
	Not Successful	4	25	29
	Total	53	147	200
Technical Knowledge	Successful	95	74	169
	Not Successful	21	7	28
	Total	116	81	197
Reading Comprehension	Successful	144	26	170
	Not Successful	24	4	28
	Total	168	30	198
Individual Attributes	Successful	26	145	171
	Not Successful	5	24	29
	Total	31	169	200

Note: "Indicator Name" refers to the SmarterMeasure Indicators. "Successful" in the Final Grade Earned column is based on the Institutional benchmark of earning a 70% or higher (A, B, or C letter grade). "Not Successful" is based on the Institutional benchmark of earning a 69% or lower (D or F letter grade).

*Reading Rate and Typing Speed are statistically significant, $\alpha = .05$, while the other SmarterMeasure Indicators are not statistically significant, $\alpha = .05$.

Reading Rate Success Compared to Final Grade Success

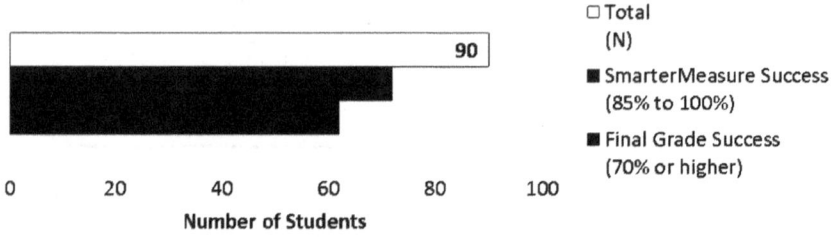

Figure 1. Reading rate success comparison

Typing Speed Success Compared to Final Grade Success

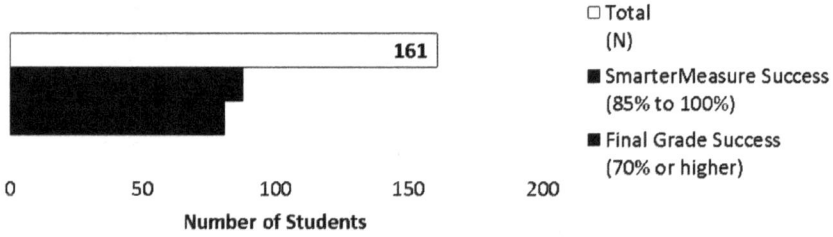

Figure 2. Typing speed score comparison

Life Factors Success Compared to Final Grade Success

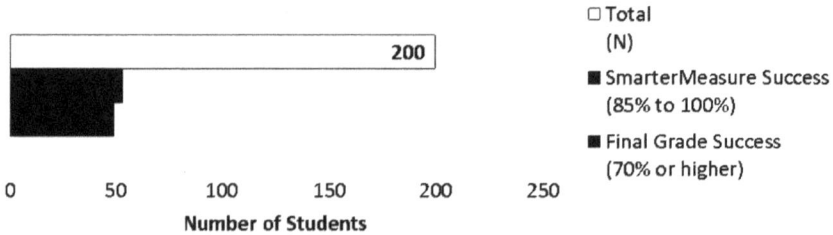

Figure 3. Life factors score comparison

Technical Knowledge Success Compared to Final Grade Success

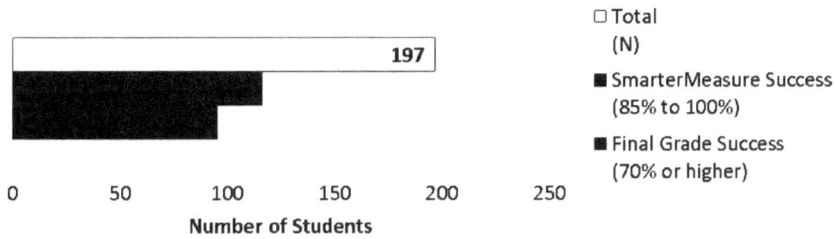

- □ Total (N)
- ■ SmarterMeasure Success (85% to 100%)
- ■ Final Grade Success (70% or higher)

Number of Students

Figure 4. Technical knowledge score comparison

Reading Comprehension Success Compared to Final Grade Success

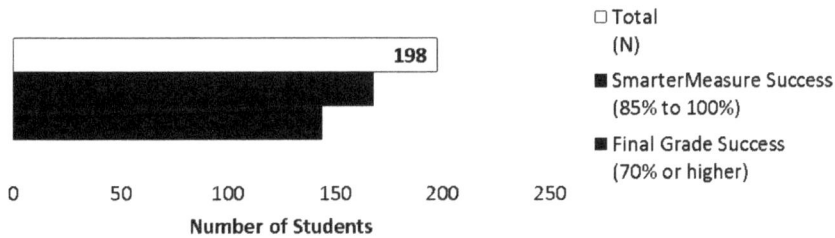

- □ Total (N)
- ■ SmarterMeasure Success (85% to 100%)
- ■ Final Grade Success (70% or higher)

Number of Students

Figure 5. Reading comprehension score comparison

Individual Attributes Success Compared to Final Grade Success

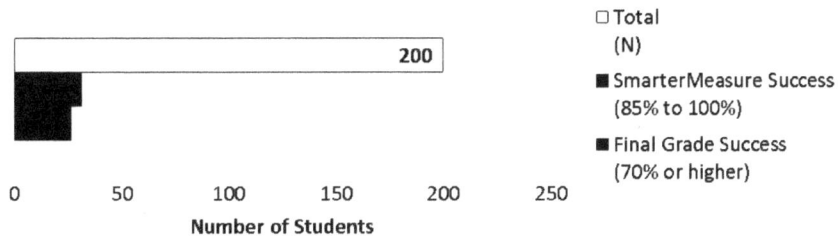

- □ Total (N)
- ■ SmarterMeasure Success (85% to 100%)
- ■ Final Grade Success (70% or higher)

Number of Students

Figure 6. Individual attributes score comparison

by student readiness factors, including individual attributes (such as motivation), life factors, learning styles, technical competency, technical knowledge, reading rate and recall, and typing speed and accuracy. Based on the results of the study, most of our hypothesis was not supported.

Only two of the SmarterMeasure indicators (Reading Rate and Typing Speed) were statistically significant, thereby exerting an influence of student readiness on student success in these particular online courses. There are two limitations to consider. First, the sample size was small. Second, there can be alternative interpretation for these results. For example, a higher typing speed with accuracy may be indicative of a student's expertise with computer technology. A higher typing speed with accuracy may also be indicative of a student's attention to detail, and it is the attention to detail factor that exerted an influence on student success. An additional possibility is that higher typing speeds were developed from experience in previous online courses, and success in previous online courses has been identified as a predictor of success (Boston, Ice, & Burgess, 2012). The possible impact of previous student success in online courses was not explored during this study and would be an additional source for correlation in readiness.

In this controlled study, two indicators (Life Factors and Technical Knowledge) were not statistically significant unless the alpha level is lowered from $\alpha = .05$ to $\alpha = .01$. The last two indicators (Reading Comprehension and Individual Attributes) were not statistically significant. The small sample size may have affected the results. An important caveat from this study is that these findings come from students in courses that meet quality standards for course design and were taught by experienced, engaging online instructors. It could

be important to further explore the impact of quality course design and engaging faculty on student readiness factors, especially those identified by SmarterMeasure.

Our findings differ from the Argosy University study, "SmarterServices" (2011). The Argosy study found the following SmarterMeasure indicators have statistically significant impact on student success: technical competency, motivation, availability of time, and retention (SmarterServices). Two factors may have contributed to the different findings. First, our small sample size may have affected our results compared to the Argosy study. Second, our study controlled for the course design, teaching, and LMS variables compared to the Argosy study; therefore, our results may be more focused.

The current study allowed a closer analysis of student readiness by controlling three variables: (a) the course design was considered high quality, as only courses that had previously met QM standards were used; (b) the LMS utilized was industry-standard and was familiar to students and instructor; and (c) the faculty participating in the study have strong, positive track records of student engagement, and were highly trained in the LMS and instructional design. We caution generalization of these findings to conclude that only typing speed/accuracy and reading rate/recall are important to the successful completion of an online course.

Suggestions for Future Research

The sample size could be broadened to increase validity and reliability, thereby leading to institutional policy changes, such as a mandatory student orientation course or standardized modules for all online courses that incorporate resources for typing and/or reading rate practice. The study could be easily replicated for extended statistical analysis using our methodology or utilizing other designs, such as a matched pair design. Another approach to increase the sample size would be to expand the study to multiple institutions/instructors with similar characteristics as the original institution in the first study. We would alert future researchers to control the inputs of quality course design and experienced, engaging online instructors.

This study was quantitative. Qualitative information could be gathered and analyzed (1) to discover other indicators of student success and (2) to test alternative analyses. For example, students who complete the SmarterMeasure instrument, perhaps as an online learning orientation (Koehnke, 2013), may be more likely to complete class work leading to student success compared to the students who elect not to complete the required SmarterMeasure instrument. Focus groups of student participants in a replicated study would add additional depth to any findings, as would using educational analytics to determine if any correlations exist between students previous online course success and readiness factors.

Another avenue of study would be to explore the actions of experienced, engaging online instructors teaching of the courses. It could be enlightening to learn if the highly skilled online instructors in this study mitigated the impact of the four other readiness factors measured that were not found statistically significant (life factors, individual attributes, technical knowledge, and reading comprehension). The findings could reveal a snapshot of pedagogical habits that promote student success in the online classroom.

The data for Life Factors and Individual Attributes indicate that a large number of students ranked at the 0% to 84% level. In this study of the 200 students, 147 ranked within 0% to 84% for Life Factors, while 53 ranked at the upper level and 169 ranked within 0% to 84% for Individual Attributes, while 39 ranked at the upper level. A future study could compare these online student rankings with students taking comparable courses using other delivery methods (e.g., face-to-face, web-hybrid). The results should also be compared to success factors in different disciplines using a matched pair experiment. For example, how does an English course, where reading comprehension is critical, compare to courses in other disciplines.

In addition, future studies could compare results from QM-certified courses to courses that have not been designed using QM standards. Likewise, a study could compare the results of less experienced with those of higher-skilled, experienced online instructors.

References

Adkins, (2013, April 25). Concerning online learning: Experience matters [Web log post]. Retrieved from http://wcetblog.wordpress.com/2013/04/25/experience matters/

Allen, M., Omori, K., Burrell, N., Mabry, E., & Timmerman, E. (2013). Satisfaction with distance education. In M. G. Moore (Ed.), *Handbook of distance education* (3rd ed., pp. 143–154). New York, NY: Routledge.

Aman, P. R. (2009). *Improving student satisfaction and retention with online instruction through systematic faculty peer review of courses.* (Unpublished doctoral dissertation). Oregon State University, Corvallis, OR. Retrieved from http://ir.library.oregonstate.edu/xmlui/bitstream/handle/1957/11945/Aman_Dissertation.pdf

Battalio, J. (2009). Success in distance education: Do learning styles and multiple formats matter? *American Journal of Distance Education*, 23(2), 46-60. doi:10.1080/08923640902854405

Boston, W., Ice, P., & Burgess, M. (2012). Assessing student retention in online learning environments: a longitudinal study. *Online Journal of Distance Learning Administration*, 15(2). Retrieved from http://www.westga.edu/~distance/ojdla/summer152/boston_ice_burgess152.pdf

Boston, W. E., Ice, P., & Gibson, A. M. (2011). Comprehensive assessment of student retention in online learning environments. *Online Journal of Distance Learning Administration*, 4(1). Retrieved from http://www.westga.edu/~distance/ojdla/spring141/boston_ice_gibson141.pdf

Curry, R. F. (2013). Academic advising in degree programs. In M. G. Moore (Ed.), *Handbook of distance education* (3rd ed., pp. 201–215). New York, NY: Routledge.

Diaz, D., & Cartnal, R. (2006). Term length as an indicator of attrition in online learning. *Journal of Online Education*, 2(5). Retrieved from http://innovateonline.info%2Fpdf%2Fvol2_issue5%2FTerm_Length_as_an_Indicator_Of_Attrition_in_Online_Learning.pdf

Dietz-Uhler, B., Fisher, A., & Han, A. (2007). Designing online courses to promote student retention. *Journal of Educational Technology Systems*, 36(1), 105–112, doi:10.2190/ET.36.1.g

Hall, A. (2010, June). *Quality Matters Rubric as "teaching presence:" Application of CoI framework to analysis of the QM Rubric's effects on student learning.* [2009 QM Research Grant]. Presentation at the 2nd Annual Quality Matters Conference, Oak Brook, IL.

Hall, M. (2011). A predictive validity study of the Revised Mcvay Readiness for Online Learning questionnaire. *Online Journal of Distance Learning Administration*, 14(3), Retrieved from http://www.westga.edu/~distance/ojdla/fall143/hall143.html

Harkness, S., Soodjinda, D., Hamilton, M., & Bolig, R. (2011, November). *Assessment of a pilot online writing program using the QM Rubric.* Paper presented at the 3rd Annual Quality Matters Conference, Baltimore, MD.

Hilke, J. (2010). Maryland Online, executive summary. In *A "w" study, why do students take a course online? why do they withdraw?* [PDF Document]. Retrieved from http://www.marylandonline.org/sites/default/files/W-Study%20Summary%20Report.pdf

Jung, I. (2012). Learners' perceptions and opinions of quality assurance. In I. Jung and C. Latchem (eds.), *Quality assurance and accreditation in distance education and e-learning: Models, policies and research* (pp. 244–254). New York, NY: Routledge.

Jung, I., & Latchem, C. (2012). Competencies and quality assurance in distance and e-learning. In I. Jung and C. Latchem (eds.), *Quality assurance and accreditation in distance education and e-learning: Models, policies and research* (pp. 231–243). New York, NY: Routledge.

Koehnke, P. J. (2013). *The impact of an online orientation to improve community college student retention in online courses: An action research study* (Doctoral dissertation, Capella University). Retrieved from http://www.cpcc.edu/pd/resources-1/doctoral-research-group/dissertations/paul-koehnke-full-dissertation

Moore, M. G., & Kearsley, G. (2012). *Distance education: A systems view of online learning* (3rd ed.). Belmont, CA: Wadsworth.
Naidu, S. (2013). Instructional design models for optional learning. In M. G. Moore (Ed.), *Handbook of distance education* (3rd ed., pp. 268–281). New York, NY: Routledge.

Pittenger, A., & Doering, A. (2010). Influence of motivational design on completion rates in online self-study pharmacy-content courses. *Distance Education*, 31(3), 275–293.

Poellhuber, B., Roy, N., & Anderson, T. (2011). Distance students' readiness for social media and collaboration. *The International Review of Research in Open and Distance Learning*, 12(6), 102–125. Retrieved from http://www.irrodl.org/index.php/irrodl/article/view/1018/1992

Runyon, J. M. (2006). *Quality in design: Impact on student achievement.* [2005 QM Research Grant]. Unpublished final report. College of Southern Maryland, LaPlata, MD: Author.

Rutland, S. R., & Diomede, S. (2011, November). *The impact of QM course revision on withdrawal rates.* [2010 QM Research Grant]. Presentation at the 3rd Annual Quality Matters Conference, Baltimore, MD.

Sherrill, J. (2012, April). 22 variable that don't affect retention of online or dev ed courses anywhere (and a few that do). Retrieved from http://wcet.wiche.edu/wcet/docs/par/22VariablesNotAffectingRetentionofOnlineStudents_SHerrill_April18-2012.pdf

SmarterServices. (2011, December 1). SmarterMeasure research findings, results of institutional level research projects [PDF Document]. Retrieved from http://www.smartermeasure.com/smartermeasure/assets/File/SmarterMeasure%20Research%20Findings.pdf

Stavredes, T. M., & Herder, T. M. (2013). Student persistence—and teaching strategies to support it. Curry, R. F. (2013). Academic advising in degree programs. In M. G. Moore (Ed.), *Handbook of distance education* (3rd ed., pp. 155–169). New York, NY: Routledge.

Swan, K. (2012). Teaching and learning in post-industrial distance education. In M. F. Cleveland-Innes & D. R. Garrison (Eds.), *An introduction to distance education: Understanding teaching and learning in a new era* (pp. 108–134). New York, NY: Routledge.

Swan, K., Matthews, D., & Bogle, L. R. (2010, June). *The relationship between course design and learning processes.* [2009 QM Research Grant]. Presentation at the 2nd Annual Quality Matters Conference, Oak Brook, IL.

Swan, K., Matthews, D., Bogle, L. R., Boles, E., & Day, S. (2011). *Linking online course design to learning processes using the Quality Matters and Community of Inquiry Frameworks.* Unpublished report on continuing study. Springfield, IL: Authors.

Wojciechowski, A., & Palmer, L. B. (2005). Individual student characteristics: Can any be predictors of success in online classes?

Online Journal of Distance Learning Admin-istration, 8(2). Retrieved from http://www.westga.edu/~distance/ojdla/summer82/wojciechowski82.htm

Developing a Community of Practice (CoP) through Interdisciplinary Research on Flipped Classrooms

Bobbie Seyedmonir, Kevin Barry, Mehdi Seyedmonir[A]

This article describes an interdisciplinary research project that resulted from the creation of a community of practice (CoP) for faculty teaching blended and online courses at a small, historically black university. Using a flipped-classroom approach, two modules of a Principles of Biology course were redesigned. Already-created PowerPoints were converted to screencasts and homework was completed in small groups during class. Results showed that students in the flipped classroom performed better on application-type questions but showed no difference on overall test scores or on knowledge-type questions. A survey of student perceptions found that students liked the autonomy to watch content videos anytime, anywhere, and that they enjoyed the more active classroom experience. Students also noted that technical issues sometimes hindered their ability to learn; they missed the opportunity to ask questions in real time; and they did not appreciate the amount of out-of-class work this approach required. Overall, the results indicate that the flipped-classroom model has the potential to increase student learning but that it requires a more thoughtful redesign process than is suggested in popular literature on the subject.

Keywords: flipped classroom, Community of Practice (CoP), instructional design, blended courses, teaching, teaching biology, higher education

Introduction

Since the time of correspondence studies, the ideal approach to the design of distance education courses was team-based in nature (Diehl, 2013). As distance education has evolved to include the use of online learning environments, the basic premise of course design has not changed. Instead of expecting faculty to become experts in the technical aspects of online course design and content creation (e.g., developing web pages and designing interactive simulations), the team approach to online course design provides faculty access to instructional designers, programmers, web developers, etc. to assist in the development and teaching of an online course, thereby allowing the faculty to focus on content (Ko & Rossen, 2010).

At many smaller institutions, however, there are fewer resources and design staff, leaving much of the work of course design and development up to the individual faculty member. This can lead faculty to feeling overwhelmed and underprepared for the task of online course design, especially since many who are asked to teach online have no training in basic instructional practices (Baran, Correia, & Thompson, 2011). Distance education administrators at such institutions have the unenviable task of finding innovative ways to provide faculty support and development opportunities in order to build skill

---

[A] West Virginia State University

levels in designing, creating, and teaching in blended and online environments.

To deal with these challenges, our University's Center for Online Learning adopted a community of practice (CoP) model (Wenger, 1998). According to Wenger (1998), within a CoP framework, more experienced faculty (or those with more expertise in a subject area) can mentor and assist in the development of faculty who are newer to the discipline, thus alleviating the strain of understaffed instructional design departments. The purpose of West Virginia State University's (WVSU's) CoP was threefold: (1) to gather a cohort of interested faculty from a variety of disciplines to discuss and learn about different approaches to blended and online course design, (2) to develop skills and knowledge that could then be shared with the group, and (3) to work together on projects of interest.

Participants in this CoP go through a semester-long training program focusing on online teaching and course design called the Online Teaching Institute (OTI). Upon graduating from OTI, faculty continue meeting monthly to discuss and receive feedback on issues they are experiencing in their blended and online courses.

During these meetings, several faculty members from science fields shared their struggle to find a mode of instruction that would utilize blended and online approaches to teach science but also preserve the integrity of their classrooms. The flipped model of instruction seemed to be especially attractive to science faculty because (1) the transition to this mode of teaching would be relatively easy as they could utilize already-existing lecture materials and (2) they would not have to give up any class time as they familiarized themselves with the format.

However, discussions in the larger, interdisciplinary CoP indicated some skepticism as to whether a literal translation of flipped classroom (i.e., taking already-existing presentation materials and recording them and using slightly modified homework assignments as in-class activities) would be effective without implementing additional course design modifications such as inquiry- or problem-based approaches.

The result of these discussions was the creation of an interdisciplinary research team which included a biologist, an educational psychologist, and an instructional designer/technologist to study the efficacy of a literal translation of the flipped classroom design on student learning in a general education biology course.

Literature Review

Blended or hybrid learning experiences have been a common part of higher education for the past decade. A three-year study of over 1,000 U.S. colleges and universities found that roughly 46% of four-year undergraduate institutions offered blended courses (Allen, Seaman, & Barrett, 2007). However, the popularity of the flipped classroom, as brought to national attention by Bergman and Sams (2012), has seen a marked growth over the past year. While there are some slight variations of the model (e.g., Musallam, 2013), most of the available literature suggests that the basic flipped instructional model consists of recorded lecture materials which are watched by students at home and application-type questions and problems (i.e., the traditional homework) which are worked on in class (Mangan, 2013; Bergman & Sams, 2012; Topo, 2011) (see Movie 1).

On a surface level, this model appears to be relatively simple to adopt and institute. An instructor needs a computer, screen capture software (such as Camtasia, Screencast-o-matic, etc.), a headset, and a

Movie 1. The flipped classroom (Flipped Learning, 2010).

place to post videos (such as YouTube), and he/she has all the equipment and software needed to get started. In short, the flipped classroom approach has a low cost of adoption, making it relatively easy to implement.

In addition to the low cost of adoption, proponents of this model have provided testimonials and anecdotal evidence suggesting a high level of success in the flipped classroom. Students are more engaged, better able to address questions requiring application of content knowledge, and are more satisfied with the classroom experience in general (e.g., Mangan, 2013; Springen, 2013; Satullo, 2013; Flipped Learning Network, 2012). Such factors combine to make the flipped classroom very attractive to teachers, faculty, school districts, and universities that are under pressure to initiate changes that increase student learning in their classrooms.

However, the empirical research in this area is still relatively sparse. Of the research that is currently available on the subject of flipped classrooms, findings have been mixed: some researchers are reporting significant learning gains in students (Tune, Sturek, & Basile, 2013; Mason, Shuman, & Cook, 2013) and some are reporting no difference between the flipped classroom and the traditional model (Winston, 2013). Because of the relative newness of this specific pedagogical approach and the subsequent need for more empirical research focused specifically on the efficacy of flipped classroom techniques, the purpose of this research project was to (1) determine whether there is a difference in student performance in a flipped classroom versus a traditional classroom setting and (2) gauge student perceptions of the flipped classroom model and its efficacy on their learning.

Methods

Participants

The classes chosen for the flipped classroom experiment were two sections of an undergraduate Principles of Biology course taught by one of the researchers ($n = 99$). Of those enrolled, $n = 88$ completed the experiment (34% male, $n = 30$ and 66% female, $n = 58$). The comparison group for this study consisted of two sections of the Principles of Biology course from the previous fall semester ($n = 89$). The comparison group was 53% male ($n = 47$) and 47% female ($n = 42$). As this course is a general education, non-majors introductory biology course, the students were not science majors.

Design

Two sections of the Principles of Biology course taught in fall 2013 utilized the flipped instructional design. Results from learning assessment scores were then compared to data from the previous fall semester. In order to ensure the comparison groups and the flipped groups were similar in terms of prior knowledge coming into the course, ACT Science scores were compared and found to be not significantly different ($F_{(1,141)} = 0.82$, $p = 0.3667$), suggesting that student groups between the two years had similar backgrounds in science, making them comparable for the purposes of this research. Furthermore, the same book, content modules, visuals, assessments, and instructor were utilized in both the treatment and comparison groups to ensure a similarity of experience.

Procedure

The first two modules of the course, *Chemistry of Biology* and *Biological Mole-*

cules, were redesigned to support flipped instruction. The videos were recorded in advance using the programs Camtasia and Adobe Presenter. While the same Power-Point presentations were used in all sections (both flipped and comparison), the screencasts in the flipped group were cut into segments that ran between 10 and 12 minutes to prevent loss of attention due to length of the screencasts (Middendorf & Kalish, 1996). For this same reason, participants were required to watch no more than two videos before each class meeting.

The participants were given an orientation to the flipped-classroom model on the first day of class and were shown how and where to access the videos on the University's learning management system (LMS). The PowerPoint files themselves (without narration) were also posted online to allow the slides to be printed for note-taking purposes. In order to further encourage participants to watch the videos, they were required to take an online quiz covering the assigned videos' material prior to each class.

During class meetings, when lectures would typically be held, the participants were instructed to break into small groups and were given application-type problems to work through while the professor provided guidance as needed. At the end of each class, the groups were called upon to answer each of the problems they had collectively worked through, and the professor clarified answers or provided the correct answers to reinforce or correct learning. At the end of the two modules, participants submitted a study guide assignment which encompassed all the material from the videos, and the professor provided final clarification of material covered in both modules.

The two modules culminated in a final assessment of participant learning which consisted of 40 multiple choice

questions and four short answer questions. The multiple choice questions were divided into those that tested knowledge/comprehension ($n = 28$) and application/synthesis ($n = 12$), as defined by the exam question bank associated with the textbook.

In addition to the final assessment, participants were asked to complete a brief survey via surveymonkey.com that measured participant perceptions of the flipped-classroom model. This survey included questions dealing with the ease of use, their personal preferences, and their beliefs about their own learning using a flipped-classroom model. The survey included both closed and open-ended questions to allow a full range of participant responses. Participants were given extra credit for completing the survey.

Results

Results of Participant Performance Test Scores

Statistical analyses of quantitative test data were conducted using SAS statistical software using a mixed model ANOVA (Proc Mixed). Though there was no significant difference in test scores overall ($F_{(1,172)} = 0.06$, $p = 0.8079$), participants in the flipped-classroom did perform significantly better on the application/synthesis multiple choice questions ($F_{(1,167)} = 4.28$, $p = 0.0402$) (see Figure 1). There was no significant difference between scores on the knowledge/comprehension multiple choice questions ($F_{(1,167)} = 013$, $p = 0.7171$).

Results of Participant Survey

The online survey was sent to all participants ($n = 99$) due to the fact that while a participant may not have taken the final assessment, they were all exposed to the flipped-classroom approach. The response rate for the survey was 78% ($n = 77$). Demographic questions indicated that survey responders were 73% female ($n = 51$) and 27% male ($n = 19$) with 9% not responding ($n = 7$). Age of respondents broke down as 50% ($n=35$) between 18 and 20 years of age, 44% ($n = 31$) between the ages of 21 and 29, 6% ($n = 4$) over 29 years of age, and 9% ($n = 7$) not responding.

Participants' thoughts on the efficacy of flipped classroom. Participants were asked to rank their level of agreement with several statements regarding flipped classroom using a Likert-type scale of 1 – Strongly Disagree to 5 – Strongly Agree. Overall, participants indicated satisfaction with the format tending to average above the midpoint in the scale on all items related to instructional format, including items such as *I think I learned more as a result of this method* and *I felt more engaged in class when the classroom was flipped* (see Figure 2).

The role of the textbook. Additionally, participants were asked to identify when they read their textbooks in relationship to the videos. Results indicated that 33% of participants ($n = 24$) read the textbook after watching the videos, thus suggesting that the videos acted as an advanced organizer for participants. Additionally, 31% of participants ($n = 22$) claimed they did not read at all (see Figure 3).

Results of open-ended questions regarding the flipped- classroom. Participants were also asked to respond to two open-ended questions, namely (1) *Please describe what you LIKED or thought was EFFECTIVE about the flipped classroom method* and (2) *Please describe what you DID NOT LIKE or thought was INEFFECTIVE about the flipped classroom method*. Thematic analysis of these responses showed five major themes related to the flipped classroom: learner autonomy, active classroom, loss of real-time response, technology problems, and more work in the class.

Learner autonomy. One of the major themes that emerged from the participant responses was the idea of learner autonomy, or being in control of when, where, and how frequently to access video content for the course. Typical responses for this item included, *I thought the flipped classroom method was effective because I could watch it on my own time. I enjoyed the fact that I could rewind parts that I did not understand and I could rewatch the videos if necessary).*

Active classroom. The second theme that presented itself was the idea of the active classroom. Participants indicated that they enjoyed working on problems in class, some saying that *...it was great to do the homework in class because I had already seen the videos and PowerPoint, so if I had any questions I could ask them. Lecturing in the classroom just gets boring, but when we engage in the class and work together, I feel like it was easier to learn.*

Loss of real-time response. Statements such as *I did not like not being able to communicate and ask questions* represent a theme found in open-ended responses that indicated to the researchers that the loss of real-time interaction while watching the videos was uncomfortable for some participants.

Technology problems. While technical problems were not common, for those students who did experience them, they appeared to negatively impact their perceptions of learning. While difficulties ranged from Internet connectivity to computer hardware and software, the general trend was that having any technical problem at all decreased the comprehension and overall satisfaction with the format. This is not unexpected as overcoming technical support issues is part of any blended or online course.

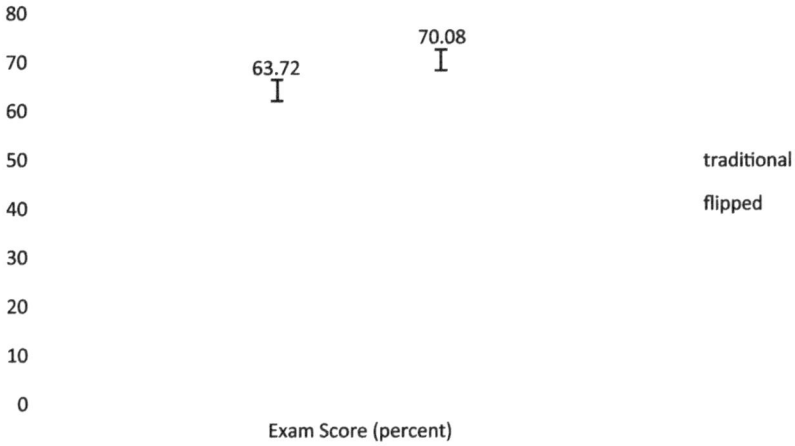

Figure 1. Mean scores on application questions.

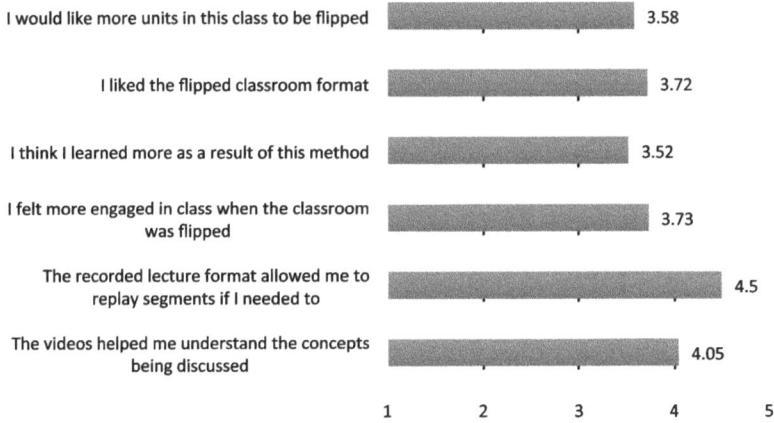

Figure 2. Mean scores of Likert-type questions.

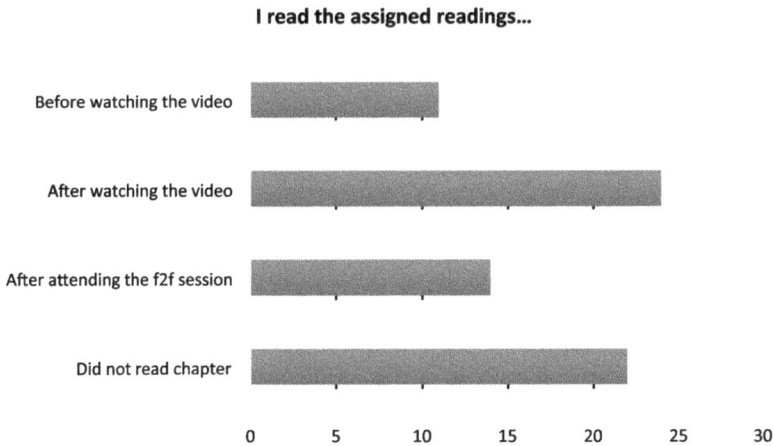

Figure 3. Counts of responses to question regarding when/if textbook was read.

More work for participants. Finally, participants indicated that they did not like the fact that the flipped- classroom design required more work from them outside of class. A representative response from this theme was: *I did not like spending so much time out of class working for the class.* While participants considered this a negative of the flipped classroom, the researchers felt this was actually a positive outcome of the flipped-classroom model.

Discussion

The results of this study seem to indicate that the flipped-classroom model has some promise as a teaching method, as participants did score significantly higher on the application portions of the learning assessment. Participants also seem to enjoy the level of autonomy they have when the course content is posted online and accessible when needed as well as the ability to play back the videos as often as needed to understand the concept. Participants also seem to enjoy the change in the nature and quality of the face-to-face components of the course as they get to spend it engaging in active learning experiences. In addition, while participants did not like the idea of having to exert more effort outside of class in the flipped classroom approach, from an instructor standpoint, participant reports of increased effort on course-related content was welcome, and might be a way to improve participant study behaviors.

However, the learning gains found are not as high as anecdotal reports suggest (e.g., Flipped Learning Network, 2012). While the flipped classroom model did lead to significant increases in test scores on application-type questions, there were no significant differences in knowledge-type questions or in overall test scores. This seems to indicate that simply flipping the class without the inclusion of other proven teaching practices such as inquiry- or problem-based approaches does not yield the greatest gains in student learning. It also might indicate that, as with so many other issues related to student content knowledge, the skill of the teacher might be a greater determinant of student learning gains than the flipping itself; however, more research is needed in these areas to determine the individual factors that lead to greater learning gains in a flipped environment.

The responses that participants provided regarding how and when they accessed textbook materials were especially interesting and suggest that the videos could be acting as an advanced organizer for the denser textbook materials. If this is the case, then the use of a quick overview video with the specific purpose of guiding reading might lead to better reading comprehension and thus greater learning gains. Further, the fact that an almost equally large number of participants did not read at all suggests that perhaps a more thoughtful evaluation of the role of textbook, and textbook alternatives, is needed in order to ensure students understand its relevancy to the course. More research on the interaction between video and textbook resources should be done to further delineate how best to interweave those two resources to optimize student learning.

There are some limitations to this study that require us to examine the findings of this research in the proper context. As the groups in this study were not randomly selected, generalization to the larger population of college students (or even college students in flipped biology courses) might be unwise. Additionally, given the amount of time that had passed between the flipped group and the comparison group (one academic year), there could be timing affects that made the groups perform differently. Further research in this area utilizing more robust research designs is warranted in order to arrive at more conclusive results about the efficacy of the flipped classroom model.

Conclusions

Research on the flipped classroom is only beginning, and, while studies on equivalency with traditional instruction are needed, more research on how and when to effectively implement this teaching strategy is the logical next step in flipped-classroom research. While this research shows that a flipped classroom can increase student learning, it does not identify which specific factors within the flipped-classroom model lead to greater learning gains in students, and further research in this area can help clarify for educators how best to incorporate this approach in their own classroom. In the end, the findings of this research seem to indicate that the flipped-classroom approach may not be the panacea for science instruction many wish it to be, but rather one more tool for a skilled instructor to use in his/her efforts to support student learning.

References

Allen, I. E., Seaman, J., & Barrett, R. (2007). Blending in: The extent and promise of online education in the U.S. Babson Research Group. Retrieved from http://sloanconsortium.org/sites/default/files/pages/Blending_In.pdf

Baran, E., Correia, A. P., & Thompson, A. (2011). Transforming online teaching practice: Critical analysis of the literature on the roles and competencies of online teachers. *Distance Education, 32*(3), 421–439. doi:10.1080/01587919.2011.610293

Bergman, J., & Sams, A. (2012). *Flip your classroom: Reach every student in every class everyday*. Washington, DC: ISTE.

Diehl, C. A. (2013). Charles A. Wedemeyer: Visionary pioneer of distance education. In Michael Moore's (ed.), *Handbook of Distance Education* (3rd ed.). New York, NY: Routledge.

Flipped Learning (2010). The flipped classroom. [YouTube video]. Retrieved from http://www.youtube.com/watch?v=2H4RkudFzlc

Flipped Learning Network. (2012). *Improve student learning and teacher satisfaction with one flip of the classroom*. Retrieved from http://flippedlearning1.files.wordpress.com/2012/07/classroomwindowinfographic7-12.pdf

Ko, S., & Rossen, S. (2010). *Teaching online: A practical guide* (3rd ed.). New York, NY: Routledge.

Mangan, K. (2013 October 4). Inside the flipped classroom. *Chronicle of Higher Education*, 60(5), B18–B21.

Musallam, R. (2013). 3 rules to spark learning [web video]. Retrieved from http://www.youtube.com/watch?v=YsYH-qfk0X2A

Mason, G. S., Shuman, T. R., & Cook, K. E. (2013). Comparing the effectiveness of an inverted classroom to a traditional classroom in an upper-division engineering course. *IEEE Transactions in Education*, 56(4), 430–435. doi:10.1109/TE.2013.2249066

Middendorf, J., & Kalish, A. (1996). The 'change-up' in lectures. *National Teaching & Learning Forum*, 5(2), 1–12. doi:10.1002/ntlf.10026

Satullo, S. K. (2013). Pa. colleges flip classrooms to boost engagement. *Community College Week, 26*(4), 13.

Springen, K. (2013). Flipping the classroom: A revolutionary approach to learning presents some pros and cons. *School Library Journal, 59*(4), 23.

Topo, G. (2011, October 7). 'Flipped' classrooms take advantage of technology. *USA Today*. Retrieved from http://usatoday30.usatoday.com/news/education/story/2011-10-06/flipped-classrooms-virtual-teaching/50681482/1

Tune, J. D. Sturek, M., & Basile, D. P. (2013). Flipped classroom model improves graduate student performance in cardiovascular, respiratory, and renal physiology. *Advanced Physiology Education, 37*, 316–320. doi:10.1152/advan.00091.2013.

Wenger, E. (1998). *Communities of practice. Learning, meaning, and identity*. Cambridge, UK: Cambridge University Press.

Winston, H. (2013). Quickwire: 'Flipping' classroom may not make much difference [web blog]. Retrieved from http://chronicle.com/blogs/wiredcampus/quickwire-flipping-classrooms-may-not-make-much-difference/47667.

Internet Learning Volume 3 Issue 1 - Spring 2014

Beliefs Regarding Faculty Participation in Peer Reviews of Online Courses

Andria F. Schwegler[A], Barbara W. Altman[B], Lisa M. Bunkowski[C]

Prior to implementing a voluntary, unofficial Quality Matters peer review process for online courses at our institution, several faculty members openly expressed concerns about the process. To systematically identify and examine how highly endorsed these beliefs actually were, we used the Theory of Planned Behavior (Ajzen, 1985) to investigate faculty beliefs and their plans to participate in the peer review. This behavior prediction model provided a logical theoretical basis for this investigation because it targets intentions to perform volitional behaviors and directly examines salient beliefs underlying attitudes, subjective norms, and perceived behavioral control toward the behavior. Though differences in belief endorsement between faculty members who chose to participate in the peer review and those who did not could not be tested statistically due to small sample sizes, a qualitative examination of the endorsement of the modal belief statements provided useful information about faculty members' perceptions of completing the peer review. Our results indicated that many of the concerns and criticisms of the peer review process were not as highly endorsed as initially assumed. Our objective examination of faculty beliefs, instead of reliance on hearsay and a vocal minority, was useful in identifying genuine faculty concerns that could be directly addressed. Our data provided directions to guide administrative changes in our process to increase participation in internal peer reviews with the goal of improving the online course design quality.

Keywords: peer review, online course design, faculty beliefs, Quality Matters, faculty attitudes

---

[A] Dr. Andria F. Schwegler is an Assistant Professor of Psychology and the Online Coordinator for the College of Education at TAMUCT. She teaches graduate and undergraduate courses in Psychology including social psychology, statistics, and research methods. Her research areas of interest include social norm formation and change, post-traumatic stress and depression symptoms in soldiers returning from combat, and the scholarship of teaching and learning.

[B] Dr. Barbara W. Altman is an Assistant Professor in Management and the Online Coordinator for the College of Business Administration at TAMUCT. She teaches graduate and undergraduate courses in Business Ethics, Leadership and Strategy. Her research interests are in corporate social responsibility, organizational change, inter-organizational partnerships, and the leadership traits necessary to facilitate such linkages. Her research interests also involve methods to improve online and blended course design and delivery.

[C] Dr. Lisa M. Bunkowski is an Assistant Professor of History and the Director of Instructional Enhancement and Innovation (IEI) at TAMUCT. She teaches graduate and undergraduate courses in American History. Her disciplinary research focus is on the mid-nineteenth century USA, with emphasis on issues of violence and gender. She is also involved with several regional Oral History projects. As the Director of IEI, she is focused on the scholarship of teaching and learning, faculty development, and is actively involved in supporting course design and delivery of online and blended programs.

Quality Matters (QM) is one of the most widely accepted set of standards guiding the online course design quality. As of 2013, QM reported over 600 member institutions, and over 22,000 faculty and instructional designers trained on the QM standards and course review process (Quality Matters, 2013). The core of the QM approach is a rubric covering eight overarching student/learner focused standards, with a total of 41 specific course design standards. To ascertain whether an online course meets these standards, a faculty developer submits a course to the faculty peer review process. The goal of this process is continuous course improvement so that any identified weaknesses are corrected, based on constructive peer feedback (Finley, 2012).

When initiating a peer review of online courses, subscribing institutions have the option to participate in either official QM reviews or unofficial internal reviews. Official QM reviews include a Master Reviewer, a Subject Matter Expert, and an external Reviewer who constitute the peer review committee, and successful completion of the process leads to the official QM designation as a quality assured course. Unofficial reviews do not receive the QM designation, but they allow institutions to select their own peer review committee members to accommodate unique institutional needs and course improvement goals. Both official QM reviews and internal peer reviews are governed by the same set of standards and consensus protocols for determining when standards are met.

The choice to participate in official versus unofficial reviews is determined at the institutional level, along with the policy of mandated versus voluntary peer review. For institutions undergoing an organizational change to implement QM, offering participation in an unofficial internal peer

review on a voluntary basis is a way to gain faculty buy-in in the process. Obviously, when participation is not optional, faculty members do not need to accept or endorse the process to prompt participation, but when the process is optional, what prompts faculty members to participate in the peer review? More specifically, what do faculty members believe about the peer review process when it is implemented at their institution? How are these beliefs related to plans to participate? How can beliefs be used to modify procedures with the goal of increasing participation rates? To provide initial answers to these questions and guide our QM implementation process, the present research investigated faculty beliefs regarding the introduction and first wave of reviews in a QM peer review process. The goal of this research was to improve our understanding of faculty beliefs regarding voluntary completion of a peer review of an online course so that revisions to our process and new institutional changes could be designed to increase faculty participation and ultimately improve our online course quality.

Literature Review

To systematically investigate faculty beliefs and plans to participate in a peer review, the Theory of Planned Behavior provided a logical theoretical basis for this study because it targets volitional behaviors and directly examines salient beliefs regarding the behavior. Ajzen's Theory of Planned Behavior (Ajzen, 1985, 1991, 2012) is one of the most widely applied behavior prediction models in the social psychology literature. In a recent reflection, Ajzen (2011) noted that the theory was cited 22 times in 1985, and citations have grown steadily to 4,550 in 2010. A review of the model's significance found this research to have the highest scientific impact score among U.S. and Canadian social psychologists (Nosek et al., 2010).

The Theory of Planned Behavior model is shown in Figure 1 (Ajzen, 2013a). The key tenets of the model include direct and indirect measures of attitudes, subjective norms, and perceived behavioral control that are used to predict intention, which subsequently predicts behavior (Ajzen, 1991, 2012, 2013a). According to this expectancy-value model, which weights beliefs about actions by their value, behavior is the actual manifestation of an individual's action in a particular circumstance. Intention is the proximal predictor of a person's behavior and indicates an individual's willingness/readiness to demonstrate that behavior. The model postulates a strong relationship between intention and behavior for those behaviors that are under one's own volitional choice. Intention is predicted from an individual's attitude toward the behavior, subjective norms regarding the behavior, and perceived behavioral control over the behavior. Attitudes are defined as "the individual's positive or negative evaluation of performing the behavior" and are assessed by having individuals respond to bipolar adjective scales regarding the behavior under examination (e.g., good–bad; Ajzen & Fishbein, 1980, p. 6). Subjective norms are "the person's perception of the social pressures put on him to perform or not perform the behavior in question" (Ajzen & Fishbein, 1980, p. 6). This social pressure is measured as a general sense of what important others think one should do. Finally, perceived behavioral control is one's sense of his or her ability to perform the behavior under examination, which can be assessed by having individuals rate the extent that performing the behavior is up to them and whether they perceive they have control over it.

Underlying these attitudes, norms, and control perceptions are one's beliefs which are weighted by the subjective value of these beliefs. Specifically, behavioral beliefs are the accessible thoughts a person holds regarding a certain behavior. These beliefs are tempered by one's evaluations of the outcomes associated with these beliefs. In terms of the model, each of a person's behavioral beliefs is multiplied by the outcome evaluation associated with that belief. Then, each of these products is summed to form an indirect assessment of one's attitude toward the behavior. In a similar manner, normative beliefs are the salient expectations perceived by individuals that are set by members of a relevant referent group (e.g., family members, co-workers). These beliefs are weighted by one's motivation to comply with these expectations, and the sum of products (i.e., each belief multiplied by the motivation to comply with it) constitutes an indirect measure of one's subjective norms regarding the behavior. Finally, control beliefs are thoughts regarding factors in the setting which may either impede or enhance the performance of the behavior. These factors are weighted by the power each control factor holds over the individual. One's level of perceived behavioral control is the sum of products (i.e., each control factor multiplied by its power of control) to perform the behavior.

Given the wide application of the theory, several notable meta-analyses speak to the model's utility in predicting intentions to engage in a multitude of behaviors. For example, in a review of 185 independent and varied applications of the model conducted prior to 1997, Armitage and Conner (2001) found that across all behaviors studied, the correlation of intention and perceived behavioral control was significant, with perceived behavioral control accounting for 27% of the variance in intention ($R^2 = 0.27$). In addition, the multiple correlations of attitude, subjective norm, and perceived behavioral control accounted for an average of 39% of the variance in intention ($R^2 = 0.39$). Their meta-analysis supported the overall efficacy of the model though they called for further study of the subjective norm component and attention to differences in self-report versus observed behavior measurement.

In a meta-analysis of 33 studies, Cooke and French (2008) examined the model's overall ability to predict intention to participate in health screenings and subsequent attendance behavior. Their meta-analysis found the strongest relationships between attitudes and intentions and the weakest relationships between subjective norms and intentions. For attendance behavior, they found a medium-sized relationship between intention and behavior and a small relationship between perceived behavioral control and behavior. These findings support the overall efficacy of the model, consistent with Armitage and Conner's findings.

In a more recent meta-analysis predicting health-related behaviors, McEachan, Conner, Taylor and Lawton (2011) analyzed 206 papers, representing 237 tests of the theory. Like previous meta-analyses, their study showed a strong relationship between intention and behavior, and perceived behavioral control predicted a small proportion of the variance in behavior. Attitude, subjective norm, and perceived behavioral control emerged as the strongest predictors of intention relative to other variables added to the model, and attitude was consistently the strongest predictor. The purpose of this research, like that of Cooke and French (2008), was to propose interventions to modify behavior that could be examined in further research. Taken together, these meta-analyses high-

light the overall efficacy of the model in behavior prediction. Unfortunately, applications of the Theory of Planned Behavior to teaching online, predicting faculty behaviors, and revising higher education practices are extremely limited. Of the few studies in this area Celuch and Slama (2002) applied the theory to a business school course to evaluate the impact of faculty-led interventions on student behavior. These researchers used pre- and post-course assessments to examine how variables in the Theory of Planned Behavior impacted learning critical-thinking skills in a marketing course. Their findings show that some variables, specifically attitudes from the Theory of Planned Behavior, were accurate predictors of changes in behavior and confirmed the positive effect of the course's pedagogy on critical thinking. Specifically, they reported that certain systematic elements of the course such as expectation setting, opportunities for practice, and constant feedback were system interventions that positively impacted observed instances of critical thinking behaviors.

Utilizing a portion of the Theory of Planned Behavior, Alshare, Kwum, and Grandon (2006) examined faculty intention to teach online at one American and two Korean institutions. Their model included two factors derived from previous research on faculty adoption of online courses, communication efficacy, and flexibility. The third factor was subjective norm taken directly from Ajzen's (1991) work. In this context, subjective norm was defined as the combined social pressure of school administrators and close faculty members to teach online courses. The hypothesis that subjective norms had a positive relationship with the adoption of online teaching was supported at both the American and Korean institutions.

More closely related to the current project, Hartmann (2011) used the Theory of Planned Behavior to explore whether institutional level interventions would alter faculty willingness to submit research grant proposals in what had been a traditional teaching institution. The hypotheses grounding the case study were derived directly from the theory and stated that a faculty member would be more likely to intend to write and actually submit a proposal for funding when that individual "believes that submitting funding proposals is a desirable and valued behavior; sees other similar people successfully writing and submitting proposals; and perceives they are able to write and submit proposals, that obstacles can be overcome" (Hartmann, 2011, p. 48).

A number of interventions were put in place to test the behavioral change regarding attitudes, subjective norms, and perceived control. For example, to change attitudes regarding submitting research grant proposals, interventions included publishing a monthly newsletter and promoting public awards and recognition. To change perceptions of subjective norms, interventions included welcome letters to new faculty and department chairs emphasizing the importance of funded research, published college-wide statistics, and faculty workload allocations. To change perceived behavioral control, grant writing workshops, how-to manuals, and tutorials were offered to faculty along with administrative support. The case study findings, documented over a 10-year period, show average annual grant proposals rising, with indirect cost support to the college increasing steadily. The case study concludes that managerial interventions can impact faculty members' intentional behaviors to increase their participation in submitting sponsored research.

The Present Research

Previous research involving the Theory of Planned Behavior supports our expectation that the model can be used to identify and measure faculty members' underlying beliefs, attitudes, subjective norms, and perceptions of control regarding voluntary decisions to participate in a peer review. As such, we used the Theory of Planned Behavior to provide a process for eliciting faculty beliefs regarding participating in a peer review as we introduced an internal QM peer review process at our institution. After the beliefs were identified, we had faculty members, those who volunteered to participate in a peer review and those who did not, evaluate the statements. Their ratings provided the basis for revisions to our procedures and for the development of interventions to increase participation in a peer review, which should subsequently improve our online course offerings.

Method

Participants

Research participation was offered to all faculty members who were eligible to participate in the peer review process during its first year of implementation (i.e., four semesters from Summer 2012 through Summer 2013). To be eligible to participate in the peer review, faculty members must have taught at least one fully online course on the recently-adopted learning management system. Of these eligible faculty members ($N = 60$), 19 faculty members volunteered to participate in the peer review process for at least one course. Of these peer review participants, eight faculty members also volunteered to participate in this research, a 42% participation rate. Of the 41 faculty members who chose not to participate in the peer review, six faculty members volunteered to participate in this research, a 15% participation rate.

Though participation in the peer review process was incentivized with a $1000 stipend for successful completion, participation in this research study was not incentivized. Faculty members received no compensation for their participation in this research, which was entirely voluntary and was not linked to peer review outcomes. The researchers, who worked with faculty members on their peer reviews, were blind to the research participation status of all faculty members until the peer review process was concluded at the end of its first year. This research was reviewed and approved by the Institutional Review Board of Texas A&M University Central Texas.

Pilot Questionnaire

Utilizing the Theory of Planned Behavior requires the development of a survey questionnaire that is based on the salient attitudes, subjective norms, and perceptions of control regarding the behavior for the target group. Therefore, the initial step in developing our primary questionnaire was documenting faculty comments and beliefs regarding the introduction of the peer review process.

Prior to implementing our internal peer review, many faculty members openly expressed concern about the process and were reluctant to participate. The only previous experience the majority of our faculty members had with a similar process was when department chairs visited their classrooms to complete their administrative faculty evaluations. These faculty evaluations tend to be stress-provoking events for most faculty members because the outcomes of the observations are directly associated with contract renewals and merit raises. So, when the peer review was discussed at our institution, many faculty members equated it with an administrative review and were not receptive.

Among the criticisms initially targeted at the peer review of online courses were claims that the comments regarding course revisions made during the context of peer review would be an infringement on the faculty course developer's academic freedom. In addition, faculty members who had previous experience with only a review of their teaching (i.e., evaluation of course delivery) were not familiar with distinguishing between course design and course delivery and held persistent beliefs that confounded the two concepts.

Faculty-generated concerns and criticisms of the peer review process were consistently directed to the Online Coordinators (i.e., faculty members who carried administrative duties to work with faculty to teach online), who were responsible for introducing and explaining the process to the faculty in their respective colleges. Immediately prior to implementation, the Online Coordinators recorded this information on a pilot questionnaire, which was used to create the main survey for this research. The behavior targeted in both the pilot questionnaire and the main survey was defined as "completing the TAMUCT peer review process for one online course by the end of the current semester." The pilot questionnaire included three, open-ended items to elicit behavioral outcomes mentioned by faculty members (i.e., advantages and disadvantages of completing the peer review and "what else comes to mind when you think about" completing this process). Normative referents for the peer review process were elicited with four open-ended questions that requested a list of the individuals or groups who would approve, disapprove, be most likely to complete, and be least likely to complete this process. Perceived behavioral control regarding the peer review process was elicited with two, open-ended items that requested a list of any factors or circumstances that would make it easy and difficult to complete the internal peer review.

Each Online Coordinator independently responded to the pilot survey with the concerns and comments that faculty members in the respective college made. The surveys were collected approximately one week after being distributed and the responses compiled. Similar comments were combined (e.g., "I will learn some new techniques for online teaching" and "See what others are doing…so I can borrow good ideas"), and some comments were reworded to communicate a neutral affective tone (e.g., "People who want to get out of the required training"). All faculty comments that were listed by the Online Coordinators on the pilot survey were represented on the final survey as a set of modal faculty beliefs. The combined, revised list of behavioral beliefs that were expressed by faculty members when the peer review process was introduced are listed in the first column of Table 1, the normative beliefs are listed in the first column of Table 2, and the control beliefs are listed in the first column of Table 3. Few control beliefs were elicited by the pilot study so these beliefs were supplemented with example items from Ajzen (2013b).

Final Peer Review Survey

The final survey consisted of 79 items assessing each of the constructs proposed by the Theory of Planned Behavior. This "Peer Review of Online Courses: Opinion Survey" included six statements that were direct measures of faculty members' attitudes toward completing the peer review process rated on 7-point scales ranging from 1 (*extremely good*) to 7 (*extremely bad*), 1 (*valuable*) to 7 (*worthless*), 1 (*pleasant*) to 7 (*unpleasant*), 1 (*enjoyable*) to 7 (*unenjoyable*), 1 (*difficult*) to 7 (*easy*) (reverse scored), and 1 (*unnecessary*) to 7 (*necessary*) (reverse scored). When examining the inter-item reliability of these statements, the item assessing how necessary completing the peer review process was displayed low correlation with the rest of the items and was removed. The remaining five items were averaged into an overall measure of attitudes (Cronbach's α = 0.90). Lower scores indicate more positive attitudes toward completing the peer review.

Direct measures of norms consisted of five items. Norms indicating what most other faculty members do were measured by responses to the following items, "faculty who are similar to me will complete the peer review process" and "most faculty will complete the peer review process" on 7-point scales ranging from 1 (*definitely true*) to 7 (*definitely false*). Norms indicating social pressure to complete the peer review were measured by responses to the following items, "most of my colleagues whose opinions I value approve of me completing the peer review process" rated as 1 (*agree*) to 7 (*disagree*), "most people who are important to me think that I 1(*should*) to 7 (*should not*) complete the peer review process," and "it is expected of me to complete the peer review process" rated as 1 (*definitely true*) to 7 (*definitely false*). When examining the inter-item reliability of these statements, the items regarding "faculty who are similar to me will" and "it is expected of me to" complete the peer review process produced low correlations with the rest of the items and were removed. The remaining three items were averaged into an overall measure of norms (Cronbach's α = 0.69). Lower scores indicate more supportive norms regarding completing the peer review.

Direct measures of perceived behavioral control were assessed by four items, including "I am confident that I can complete the peer review process" and "I have full control over whether I complete the process" rated as 1 (*definitely true*) to 7 (*definitely false*). One item assessed agreement with the statement that "whether or not I complete the peer review process is completely up to me" 1 (*strongly agree*) to 7 (*strongly disagree*), and one item measured whether completing the peer review process is 1 (*impossible*) to 7 (*possible*) (reverse scored). When examining the inter-item reliability of these statements, the item assessing how possible completion of the peer review process was displayed low correlation with the rest of the items and was removed. The remaining three items were averaged into an overall measure of perceived control (Cronbach's α = 0.72). Lower scores indicate more perceptions of control over completing the peer review process.

Intention to complete the peer review process for one online course by the end of the current semester was assessed by four items. Participants rated the following statements, "I plan to complete the process" on a 1 (*extremely likely*) to 7 (*extremely unlikely*) scale, "I will make an effort to complete the process" on a 1 (*definitely will*) to 7 (*definitely will not*) scale, "I intend to complete the peer review process" on a 1 (*strongly agree*) to 7 (*strongly disagree*) scale, and "I am going to complete the process" on a 1 (*definitely true*) to 7 (*definitely false*) scale. These items were averaged into an overall measure of intention (Cronbach's α = 0.99). Lower scores indicate stronger intentions to participate in the peer review process.

Research participants' past behavior in the internal peer review process since its inception was assessed with two open-ended items requesting the number of courses submitted and the number of courses successfully completing the peer review process. All but three participants had no courses reviewed through the internal peer review process prior to their participation in this research. Research participants' actual behavior regarding peer review completion was recorded at the end of the initial round of peer reviews (i.e., 15 months after the project was implemented) with a 0 (*non-participant*) and 1 (*participant*) distinction. All research participants who started the peer review process successfully completed it before the review process was closed.

Indirect measures of attitudes (i.e., behavioral beliefs and outcome evaluations), norms (i.e., normative beliefs and motivation to comply) and perceived behavioral control (i.e., control beliefs and power of control factors) were assessed with the beliefs elicited from the pilot study presented in Tables 1–3, respectively.

For the indirect measure of attitudes, each behavioral belief listed in Table 1 was written as the conclusion to the statement "Completing the TAMUCT peer review process will" and was rated on a 7-point scale from 1 (*extremely unlikely*) to 7 (*extremely likely*). The positive items phrased in terms of benefits of participating in the process (i.e., items 1 through 7) were reverse scored. Each outcome evaluation was adapted to fit as the conclusion to "For me to" and was rated on a 7-point scale from 1 (*extremely good*) to 7 (*extremely bad*). Lower scores indicate more supportive beliefs regarding completing the peer review process. Consistent with the Theory of Planned Behavior model, each behavioral belief was multiplied by the corresponding outcome evaluation prior to summing all the products for the composite indirect measure of attitudes.

For the indirect measure of norms, each normative belief listed in Table 2 was written as the subject to the statement "think(s) that I should complete the TA-MUCT peer review process for one online course by the end of the current semester" and was rated on a 7-point scale from 1 (*extremely likely*) to 7 (*extremely unlikely*). Motivation to comply with each referent was inserted in the blank "Generally speaking, how much do you care what your ___ thinks you should do" and was rated on a 7-point scale from 1 (not at all) to 7 (very much), which was reverse scored. Lower scores indicate more supportive beliefs regarding completing the peer review process. Consistent with the Theory of Planned Behavior model, each normative belief was multiplied by the corresponding motivation to comply prior to summing all the products for the composite indirect measure of norms.

For the indirect assessment of perceived behavioral control, each control belief listed in Table 3 was adapted to fit the blank "How often do you encounter ___" and was rated on a 7-point scale from 1 (*very rarely*) to 7 (*very frequently*). The items regarding receiving assistance from the Online Coordinator and receiving incentives to complete work were reverse scored. To assess the power of control factors, each control belief was inserted at the beginning of the statement "it would make it more difficult (or easier as noted in Table 3) for me to complete the TAMUCT peer review process for one online course by the end of the current semester" and was rated on a 7-point scale from 1 (*strongly agree*) to 7 (*strongly disagree*). All items were reverse scored except the items regarding receiving assistance from the Online Coordinator and receiving incentives to complete work.

Lower scores indicate more supportive beliefs regarding completing the peer review process. Consistent with the Theory of Planned Behavior model, each control belief was multiplied by the corresponding power of control factor prior to summing all the products for the composite indirect measure of perceived behavioral control.

Procedure

Our recently independent, regional university began offering online courses in Fall 2009 and became a QM-subscribing institution in Fall 2010. Concurrently, the institution submitted our "Institutional Plan for Distance Education" to the state's Higher Education Coordinating Board, outlining 17 fully online programs to be implemented over three years. During this high online growth period, University leadership was committed to providing institutional supports (e.g., training, incentives, mentors) to faculty to design high quality courses and put in place a culture where online quality was valued. In support of this goal, the Online Coordinator (OC) position was created in which one faculty member from each college assumed part-time administrative duties to facilitate and mentor faculty teaching online courses. All OCs were QM Certified Peer Reviewers and taught fully online courses. As our procedures evolved, QM training was made mandatory for faculty teaching online courses, and submitting a course for peer review became a voluntary but incentivized option. The University's QM goal was that as many faculty as possible would submit their courses for peer review so that course improvements could achieve design quality as demonstrated through meeting QM standards. By summer 2012, we had trained 56 of our faculty members on the QM Rubric when we introduced our peer review process.

The decision to develop an internal process at our institution, rather than adopt the official QM process, was based on a consensus of faculty preference. Our faculty wanted to be personally engaged in the peer review process, and they were reluctant to involve external reviewers, whom they believed might not understand our unique institution. In addition, some faculty members expressed concern about a pre-existing, external procedure being "imposed" upon them. To gain faculty support, we tailored our peer review process to allow faculty ownership of it and reassure them that they would have the chance to revise their courses before any official reviews were undertaken.

In our process, faculty members intending to submit a course for peer review made the request through the Distributed Learning and Instructional Technology Office, which informed the respective college OC. During the initial contact with the faculty member, the OC invited the faculty member to participate in this research study. Potential participants received a copy of the IRB approved Informed Consent form and a link to the online survey administered via Survey Monkey. Faculty members were instructed to return the signed Informed Consent form to a designated staff member in the institution's research office, not to the OC, and then complete the online survey. Because each OC collaborated as a facilitator and mentor with each peer review participant on course revisions prior to the course being submitted to the internal peer review team, all OCs were blind to the research participation status until all peer reviews were completed.

To initiate the review process, the faculty course developer conducted a self-review of the course using the QM Rubric by identifying the location in the course where each standard was met. The purpose of the self-review was to get faculty familiar with using the Rubric as a peer review tool and allow them to systematically examine their course from a reviewer's perspective to reduce their apprehension and assist them in making revisions to the course before revealing it to the peer review team. While the faculty course developer completed the self-review, the faculty member's college OC conducted an independent review of the course. After the faculty course developer and the OC completed their reviews, they met to discuss revisions to the course. Faculty members were under no obligation to implement any of the revisions suggested by the OC, who served strictly in a support role to assuage faculty concerns regarding administrative evaluation. Once the faculty course developer was satisfied with the course, it was opened to the peer review team.

To be eligible to serve for an internal peer review team, each reviewer completed the Applying the Quality Matters Rubric course (APPQMR), the established, basic QM Rubric course. Once the review teams were set and the course opened to the peer review team, the OC stepped out of the process, and the faculty Chair of the review team was responsible for scheduling timelines, leading team meetings, and closing the review in the QM Course Review Management System. The peer review was conducted in accordance with the official QM process and met/not met numbering thresholds. If the course did not meet the threshold requirements on the initial review, the faculty course developer consulted with the peer review team and made revisions to the course until it earned enough points to meet requirements. Eligible faculty members received a $1,000 stipend when their courses successfully completed the entire peer review process, and these courses were distinguished as internally quality assured. As part of the transition when training to teach online became mandatory, prior successful completion of the peer review was sufficient evidence of online course development proficiency to exempt a faculty member from taking the required training to teach online, which rendered the faculty member ineligible for the incentive. Faculty members who volunteered to peer review courses also received a small stipend (i.e., $250 for every three courses reviewed).

At the close of the fourth and final semester of peer reviews following this procedure, each college OC sent an email invitation to participate in this research study to the faculty members identified as eligible to submit a course for peer review but who choose not to participate. These individuals received an electronic copy of the Informed Consent form and a link to the online survey. They were instructed to return the signed Informed Consent form to the staff member in the institution's research office prior to completing the online survey. Research participation was closed for all faculty members at the beginning of the Fall 2013 semester.

Results

The means and standard deviations for each behavioral belief and outcome evaluation rated by faculty members during the introduction of the internal peer review process are listed in Table 1 by the peer review participation status. Each belief was multiplied by its outcome evaluation, and all products were summed to compute the indirect measure of attitude.

The means and standard deviations for each normative belief and motivation to comply rated by faculty members during the introduction of the internal peer review process are listed in Table 2 by the peer review participation status. Each belief was multiplied by its motivation to comply, and all products were summed to compute the indirect measure of subjective norms.

The means and standard deviations for each control belief and power of the control factor rated by faculty members during the introduction of the internal peer review process are listed in Table 1 by the peer review participation status. Each belief was multiplied by its power of control factor, and all products were summed to compute the indirect measure of perceived behavioral control.

The means and standard deviations for the direct and indirect measures of attitudes, norms, perceived behavioral control, and intention are presented in Table 4. Group means by the peer review completion status are also presented. All participants who submitted a course to the peer review successfully completed the process by the end of the 15-month data collection period.

The correlation coefficients among direct and composite indirect measures of attitudes, norms, control, intentions, and behavior are presented in Table 5. When examining the relationship between the direct assessments of attitudes, norms, and control with the indirect assessments of these constructs, respectively, only the two measures of attitude were highly correlated for this small sample. The direct measure of attitudes was positively correlated with the composite indirect measure of attitudes. The direct measure of norms was not highly correlated with the indirect measure of norms, and the direct measure of perceived behavioral control was not highly correlated with the indirect measure of control.

Additional analyses including multiple regression that were planned could not be computed due to the small sample size.

Discussion

Though differences between participants' and nonparticipants' belief endorsement could not be tested statistically due to unexpectedly small sample sizes, a qualitative examination of the endorsement of the modal belief statements provides some useful information about faculty members' perceptions of completing the peer review. Analyzing the data with a qualitative lens after quantitative analysis conforms with mixed method approaches that point out the advantages of complementarity, in which the alternative method can enhance or clarify the results from the initial method used, leading to an improved understanding of the phenomenon under study (Greene, Caracelli, & Graham 1989; Johnson & Onwuegbuzie, 2004; Molina-Azorin, 2012).

When measured directly, both participants in the internal peer review process and those who did not participate held relatively positive attitudes toward completing the peer review (see Table 4), an unexpected outcome given the reluctance and skepticism expressed by some faculty members when the process was introduced. Of course, these positive attitudes may not be representative of those held by all faculty members given that those who held the most negative attitudes may have refused to participate in the peer review and this research. But, if these negative attitudes remain for some, they were not pervasive to affect all faculty members.

For our sample, consistent with the direct measures of attitudes, the behavioral beliefs underlying participants' and nonparticipants' attitudes regarding the peer review process were positive (see Table 1). Both groups believed that completion of the peer review would allow them to improve their courses, learn new techniques, and gain a better understanding of the quality. Both groups indicated moderately positive beliefs that completion of the peer review would be useful in their promotion and tenure packets and would help other faculty members improve their courses. Nonparticipants were more likely to believe that the peer review would be effortful and time consuming than participants in the process. Initial concerns regarding faculty not getting along and infringement on academic freedom were not highly endorsed by either group. Both groups agreed that these outcomes would be bad, but neither group believed that these outcomes were very likely. Neither group held strong beliefs that the peer review process would be confusing or require changes that they did not want to make to their courses.

Regarding norms, on the direct measure, both participants in the peer review process and those who did not participate held beliefs supportive of completing the peer review process (see Table 4). Examining this scale by item, both participants and nonparticipants thought that valued colleagues (participants $M = 2.25$, $SD = 1.17$; nonparticipants $M = 2.00$, $SD = 1.10$) and important people (participants $M = 2.25$, $SD = .71$; nonparticipants $M = 1.50$, $SD = 1.00$) would approve of them completing the peer review process. However, when asked whether most faculty members will complete the peer review process, both participants ($M = 4.13$, $SD = 2.10$) and nonparticipants ($M = 4.50$, $SD = 1.05$) failed to acknowledge this item as definitely true. This is not a surprising outcome given that peer review of online courses had just been introduced.

Consistent with direct measures of norms, the normative beliefs underlying participants' and nonparticipants' perceptions regarding the peer review process and their motivations to comply with normative referents were supportive of completing the peer review (see Table 2). Both participants and nonparticipants believed that Department Heads, Online Coordinators, School Directors (i.e., Deans), the distance learning office personnel, and administrators in the Provost's office supported completion of the peer review process, and faculty members were motivated to comply with these referents. However, colleagues, those who teach online and those who do not, were less likely to be endorsed as sources of support for completion of peer review, and faculty were less motivated to comply with these referents. This is a paradoxical finding because colleagues who teach online are the peers who are performing the peer review of courses. Similarly, both participants and nonparticipants did not believe it was likely that students would think they should complete a peer review of an online course, though faculty members indicated that they did care what students thought they should do. Paradoxically, students are the direct beneficiaries of a course improved by a peer review, but faculty members did not believe that students thought they should complete one.

Regarding perceived behavioral control, on the direct measure, participants in the peer review process were less likely than nonparticipants to agree that completing the peer review was entirely up to them and that they had full control over it (see Table 4). It appears that the participants acknowledged that the peer reviewers would have some control over the process. Nonparticipants in the peer review indicated more control over (not) completing the process.

On the indirect perceived behavioral control items, both nonparticipants and participants in the peer review acknowledged that unanticipated demands on their time were frequent and would make it difficult to complete the peer review (see Table 3). But, the two groups held divergent beliefs on several control related items. Nonparticipants reported more frequent problems using the learning management system, more family obligations, more employment demands, and more feelings of being ill that would make it difficult to complete the peer review process than did participants. Both groups indicated that disagreements with colleagues were rare, but if they occurred, peer review participants thought these disagreements would make it more difficult to complete the peer review process than did nonparticipants. Those who did not participate in the peer review thought that having assistance from the Online Coordinator would make it easier to complete the process. Those who chose to participate in the peer review were already working with the Online Coordinator to start the process but reported less reliance on the Online Coordinator. Neither group reported that incentives to complete work were frequent, but both groups acknowledged that incentives would make completing the peer review process easier, particularly the nonparticipants, though completion of the peer review process was already incentivized.

Not surprisingly, participants in the peer review process indicated stronger intentions to complete the process than did nonparticipants. Participants also indicated less variability in their intentions than did nonparticipants, who responded less consistently regarding their intentions to complete the process (see Table 4).

Implications

Looking at our research results as a whole, many of the initial concerns and criticisms of the peer review process were not as highly endorsed as initially assumed.

An objective examination of faculty beliefs, instead of reliance on hearsay and a vocal minority, was useful in identifying genuine faculty concerns that can be directly addressed. Consistent with the previous research, most notably Hartman (2011) who used the Theory of Planned Behavior to design interventions geared to changing behaviors, our data suggest some initial directions to guide administrative changes in our process.

Based on this research, we are revising the delivery of our process in an attempt to increase participation in our internal peer review. Despite institutional recognition and monetary incentives, the majority of faculty members at our institution chose not to participate in the peer review. Apparently, institutional supports alone are not sufficient when introducing the peer review to faculty members who have experienced only administrative reviews of teaching. We are exploring additional ways to support faculty participation in peer reviews. For example, as indicated in this research, limited faculty time and perceived difficulty of completing the process were concerns endorsed by faculty. Therefore, we are examining how we can link our required training to teach online with our peer review process to consolidate what faculty members perceive as two distinct processes with different goals. Though both the prerequisite training to develop a course so that it can be taught online and the peer review performed after the course has been taught at least once share the same goals of course development and revision, our faculty do not necessarily view the processes as related. By incorporating the peer review process with the conclusion of the required training, course development and revision in the light of the QM standards would be a direct application of training. Linking the processes would allow faculty to utilize

near transfer of learning from training and make it clear that course development is the goal instead of merely completing trainings to gain the ability to teach online and then participating in a peer review if time permits. Consolidation of the faculty workload may create the perception of one process that is directly applicable to their primary responsibilities. Related to this issue, we also intend to reframe our QM training and course development activities to better emphasize their linkage to improved student learning. The finding that our faculty perceived that students would not desire their involvement in the peer review was concerning, given that the foundational element of the process is improving courses so that student learning improves. We think that understanding this linkage is critical to fostering faculty buy-in to the process.

To demonstrate to faculty that peer review is a valid use of their limited time and that their effort will produce visible results, we are planning to showcase peer reviewed courses as model course exemplars for other faculty. It is our goal to create a teaching and learning community in which faculty members openly share course improvement ideas. If effective, this practice may increase the incentive to participate in peer reviews without increasing the cost of the process. We are currently hosting faculty brown bags to set the conditions and are drafting a plan to establish a new peer-to-peer mentoring program to support our peer review process.

Another revision to our internal procedures with the goal of increasing peer review participation is increasing the incentive to become a peer reviewer. Though we had several faculty member volunteers to review courses even before we included a small stipend, a small group of faculty members shouldered a heavy review workload. Expanding our pool of trained internal peer reviewers will increase the level of training of our faculty overall and better distribute the course review workload. An alternative to alleviating our staffing limitations is to shift to external peer reviews once faculty members have a better understanding and buy-in of the peer review process.

Future Research

Two additional research streams are suggested by this initial study. The first is expansion of the original project to include other institutions that are at a similar point in QM implementation (i.e., hosting voluntary, internal peer reviews) to increase the available participant pool. Initially, after we identified and assessed faculty members' beliefs, we planned to test the utility of attitudes, norms, and perceived behavioral control in predicting faculty intention to participate in the peer review and then predict actual behavior from intention. However, at the close of our data collection period when the researchers were no longer blind to the research participation status of our peer review participants, we realized that our sample size was too small to support such an examination. A power analysis confirmed this concern. Given the R^2 from the current dataset (i.e., $R^2 = 0.32$), a sample size of at least 34 participants would be needed for a test of the model with power = 0.90 and α = 0.05 (Cohen & Cohen, 1983). Though our total number of eligible faculty members was large enough to support such a test, we were not able to recruit enough participants for this entirely voluntary, un-incentivized research study. With a larger sample of faculty who are being introduced to the QM peer review at other institutions, a broader picture of the accommodations that are made to the process to gain faculty buy-in could be obtained. In addition, given that

norms are group-specific expectations, groups of faculty members may hold different norms at other institutions. Conducting this study on a larger set of institutions would allow for more general statements regarding faculty beliefs and motivations to comply with expectations regarding the peer review of courses. Such research may also shed light on the direction that norms and attitudes shift as faculty members embrace peer review as a method of continuous course improvement.

A second stream of research will be directed at improving the feedback provided during the course of internal peer reviews. A cursory review of comments provided to faculty course developers at the close of this initial set of internal reviews revealed substantial inconsistencies across reviewers. Given that we firmly believe that internal peer review is a tool that is helping our institution build a culture of continuous course improvement, promoting more rigorous standards for acceptable reviewer comments may have the potential to more efficiently improve the course quality. To evaluate this prediction, this research team is planning to systematically examine the content of the comments provided by our peer reviewers to evaluate the extent that feedback provided to faculty course developers was consistent with the QM training that reviewers received (e.g., that reviewers referenced specific Rubric standards and provided evidence from the course). The results of this research will shed light on the nature of comments that peer reviewers make and suggest areas for revision of training and minimum content standards for comments. Follow-up research is planned to determine whether revisions of training and comment standards positively affect the content of reviewer comments and assist faculty course developers in improving their courses.

Conclusion

In this paper we have presented a preliminary research study using the Theory of Planned Behavior, a well-supported model of behavior prediction, to examine beliefs that underlie faculty participation in the peer review of online course design quality. While the results of this study were limited due to the small sample size, the qualitative interpretations presented lead to both refinements in our institutional processes and avenues for future research. Online course quality is an important goal, not only in our newly independent University with a rapidly growing online presence, but in all institutions of higher education with online programs. Peer review and use of an established benchmark, like the QM Rubric, command scientific inquiry to improve their application. The findings of this study are an important first step to this ongoing line of inquiry.

References

Ajzen, I. (1985). From intentions to actions: A theory of planned behavior. In J. Kuhl & J. Beckman (Eds.), *Action-control: From cognition to behavior* (pp. 11-39). Heidelberg: Springer.

Ajzen, I. (1991). The theory of planned behavior. *Organizational Behavior and Human Decision Processes*, 50, 179-211.

Ajzen, I. (2011). The theory of planned behaviour: Reactions and reflections. *Psychology & Health*, 26(9), 1113-1127. doi: 10.1080/08870446.2011.613995

Ajzen, I. (2012). The theory of planned behavior. In P.A.M. Lange, A. W. Kruglanski, & E.T. Higgins (Eds.), *Handbook of theories of social psychology*, 1, 438-459. London: Sage.

Ajzen, I. (2013a). *Icek Ajzen TBP Diagram*. Retrieved November 25, 2013 from http://people.umass.edu/aizen/tpb.diag.html

Ajzen, I. (2013b). *Sample TBP Questionnaire*. Retrieved December 30, 2013 from http://people.umass.edu/aizen/pdf/tpb.questionnaire.pdf

Ajzen, I., & Fishbein, M. (1980). *Understanding attitudes and predicting social behavior*. Englewood Cliffs, NJ: Prentice-Hall.

Alshare, K., Kwum, O., & Grandon, E. (2006). Determinants of instructors' intentions to teach online courses: A cross-cultural perspective. *The Journal of Computer Information Systems*, 46(2), 87-95.

Armitage, C. J., & Conner, M. (2001). Efficacy of the theory of planned behaviour: A meta-analytic review. *British Journal of Social Psychology*, 40(4), 471-499.

Celuch, K., & Slama, M. (2002). Promoting critical thinking and life-learning: An experiment with the theory of planned behavior. *Marketing Education Review*, 12(2), 13-22.

Cohen, J., & Cohen, P. (1983). *Applied Multiple Regression/Correlation Analysis for the Behavioral Sciences* (2nd ed.). Hillsdale, NJ: Lawrence Erlbaum.

Cooke, R., & French, D. P. (2008). How well do the theory of reasoned action and theory of planned behaviour predict intentions and attendance at screening programmes? A meta-analysis. *Psychology & Health, 23*(7), 745-765.

Finley, D.L. (2012). Using Quality Matters to improve all courses. *Journal of Learning and Teaching with Technology, 1*(2), 48-50.

Greene, J. C., Caracelli, V. J., & Graham, W. F. (1989). Toward a conceptual framework for mixed-method evaluation designs. *Educational Evaluation and Policy Analysis, 11*(3), 255-274.

Hartmann, A. (2011). Case study: Applying the theory of planned behavior as interventions to increase sponsored project proposal submission from liberal arts faculty. *Journal of Research Administration, 42*(1), 46-60.

Johnson, R. B., & Onwuegbuzie, A. J. (2004). Mixed methods research: A research paradigm whose time has come. *Educational Researcher, 33*(7), 14-26. doi: 10.3102/0013189X033007014

McEachan, R.R.C., Conner, M., Taylor, N., & Lawton, R.J. (2011). Prospective prediction of health-related behaviors with the theory of planned behavior: A meta-analysis. *Health Psychology Review, 5,* 97–144. doi: 10.1080/17437199.2010.521684

Molina-Azorin, J. F. (2012). Mixed methods research in strategic management: Impact and applications. *Organizational Research Methods, 15*(1), 33-56. doi: 10.1177/1094428110393023

Nosek, B.A., Graham, J., Lindner, N.M., Kesebir, S., Hawkins, C.B., Hahn, C., . . . Tenney, E.R. (2010). Cumulative and career-stage citation impact of so-cial-personality psychology programs and their members. *Personality and Social Psychology Bulletin, 36,* 1283–1300. doi: 10.1177/0146167210378111

Quality Matters. (2013). *Quality Matters Overview.* Retrieved December 26, 2013 from https://www.qualitymatters.org/applying-rubric-15/download/QM_Overview_for%20Current%20Subscribers_AE2013.pdf

	Participants				Nonparticipants			
	Belief		Evaluation		Belief		Evaluation	
	M	SD	M	SD	M	SD	M	SD
Help me improve my course	2.00	0.93	1.13	0.35	1.50	1.22	1.00	0.00
Give me the opportunity to earn the incentive	2.63	2.20	1.63	0.92	1.83	1.33	2.17	1.47
Keep me from taking the required training	5.29	1.98	4.25	1.91	5.83	2.04	4.83	2.64
Allow me to learn some new techniques	2.57	1.27	1.25	0.46	1.83	1.60	1.17	0.41
Help me gain a better understanding of quality	2.00	0.93	1.50	1.07	2.00	2.00	1.33	0.82
Support my Promotion and Tenure packet	2.63	0.92	1.25	0.46	2.83	1.94	1.83	0.75
Allow me to help other faculty improve their courses	3.25	1.58	1.88	0.83	2.83	1.47	1.50	0.55
Be time consuming and effortful	4.88	1.36	2.88	1.55	6.00	1.55	2.67	1.37
Require changes I do not want to make	3.63	1.41	3.63	1.41	2.17	1.94	3.67	2.07
Require me to commit time that I do not have	4.63	0.74	4.13	1.25	5.17	1.72	4.83	2.04
Subject me to faculty members not getting along	2.88	1.46	5.13	1.36	2.33	1.97	6.00	1.27
Be an unfamiliar process and cause me to be confused	2.50	1.60	4.25	1.67	3.00	1.58	4.00	1.10
Be an infringement on my academic freedom	2.25	1.49	5.63	1.19	2.00	2.00	5.67	1.37

Table 1

Behavioral Beliefs and Outcome Evaluations (i.e., Indirect Assessment of Attitudes) Expressed by Faculty Members during the Introduction of the Internal Peer Review Process by Peer Review Participation

| | Participants | | | | Nonparticipants | | | |
| | Belief | | Motivation | | Belief | | Motivation | |
	M	SD	M	SD	M	SD	M	SD
My Department Head	2.00	1.07	1.57	0.79	2.67	1.97	1.67	0.52
My Online Coordinator	1.75	1.04	1.63	0.74	1.67	0.41	1.80	0.84
My colleagues who teach online	3.50	0.76	2.25	0.89	3.33	1.03	3.17	0.98
My colleagues who do not teach online	4.13	0.99	3.13	0.99	3.67	1.86	4.33	1.87
Administrators in the Provost's Office	2.75	1.58	2.13	0.99	3.00	2.00	2.17	0.75
My School (College) Director	1.88	0.99	1.71	0.76	3.17	1.83	1.83	0.75
University Distance Learning Personnel	1.50	0.76	1.75	1.04	2.33	1.97	2.50	1.38
Students	4.13	1.73	1.63	0.74	4.33	2.50	1.83	0.98

Table 2

Normative Beliefs and Motivations to Comply (i.e., Indirect Assessment of Norms) Expressed by Faculty Members during the Introduction of the Internal Peer Review Process by Peer Review Participation

| | Participants | | | | Nonparticipants | | | |
| | Belief | | Power | | Belief | | Power | |
	M	SD	M	SD	M	SD	M	SD
If I encountered unanticipated events that placed demands on my time	5.50	0.76	4.63	1.51	5.83	0.98	5.17	1.47
If I had problems using Blackboard when teaching online	2.50	1.93	4.63	1.92	3.83	1.72	5.83	2.04
If I had family obligations that placed unanticipated demands on my time	3.63	1.77	4.29	1.25	5.17	1.17	5.67	1.37
If work or employment placed unanticipated demands on my time	4.75	1.67	4.88	0.99	6.00	1.10	5.33	1.51
If I felt ill, tired, or listless	2.50	1.69	4.50	1.41	4.00	1.67	4.83	1.94
If I had information or assistance from the Online Coordinator (easier)	3.36	1.69	3.75	1.67	2.33	0.82	2.00	2.00
If I had disagreements with my colleagues	1.63	0.74	4.14	1.68	1.50	0.55	2.17	1.94
If I had monetary or other incentives (easier)	5.50	1.41	3.13	1.89	5.67	1.21	2.00	1.10

Table 3

Control Beliefs and Power of Control Factors (i.e., Indirect Assessment of Perceived Behavioral Control) Expressed by Faculty Members during the Introduction of the Internal Peer Review Process by Peer Review Participation

	Total		Participants		Nonparticipants	
	M	SD	M	SD	M	SD
Direct Attitude	2.31	1.07	1.98	0.57	2.77	1.45
Indirect Attitude	138.50	51.28	133.57	45.16	145.40	63.79
Direct Norm	2.79	0.95	2.88	1.14	2.67	0.70
Indirect Norm	55.64	30.96	48.00	29.77	64.80	33.12
Direct Control	2.14	1.20	2.54	1.40	1.61	0.65
Indirect Control	137.39	32.38	125.71	29.82	151.00	32.19
Intention	2.11	1.69	1.38	0.63	3.08	2.21

Table 4

Means and Standard Deviations for Direct and Composite Indirect Measures of Attitudes, Norms, Perceived Behavioral Control, and Intention by Peer Review Participation

	Direct Attitude	Indirect Attitude	Direct Norm	Indirect Norm	Direct Control	Indirect Control	Intention	Behavior
Direct Attitude	—							
Indirect Attitude	0.66	—						
Direct Norm	0.27	0.52	—					
Indirect Norm	0.02	0.30	0.28	—				
Direct Control	0.32	0.58	0.43	−0.03	—			
Indirect Control	0.18	0.36	−0.23	0.18	−0.24	—		
Intention	0.48	0.28	−0.16	−0.07	0.01	0.60	—	
Behavior	−0.38	−0.12	0.11	−0.28	0.40	−0.41	−0.52	—

Table 5

Correlations among Direct and Composite Indirect Measures of Attitudes, Norms, Control, Intention, and Behavior

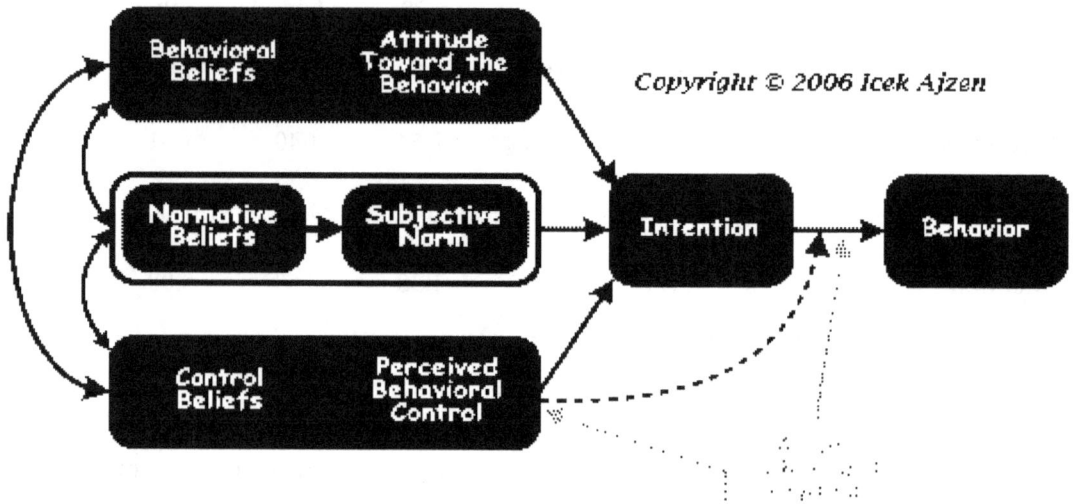

Figure 1. The Theory of Planned Behavior. The beliefs on the left of the figure are multiplied by their respective values and summed to create an indirect measure of attitudes, subjective norms, and perceived behavioral control, respectively. These beliefs and their value underlie one's attitude, subjective norm, and perceived behavioral control regarding a target behavior. One's attitude, subjective norm, and perceived behavioral control are also directly measured and predict one's intention to perform a target behavior. One's intention to perform a behavior is used to predict one's actual behavior. One's perceived behavioral control can be used to serve as a proxy for one's actual behavioral control and can be included with intention to predict behavior.

Reprinted from "TPB Diagram" by I. Ajzen, 2013a, http://people.umass.edu/aizen/faq.html. Copyright 2006 by Icek Ajzen.

Surveying Student Perspectives of Quality: Value of QM Rubric Items

Penny Ralston-Berg[A]

The Quality Matters (QM) Rubric is based on academic research. A national survey was conducted to compare QM Rubric item numerical rankings with student rankings of quality elements. Results of the survey are shared.

Keywords: online course, quality, student perspective, QM, Quality Matters, course design elements

Introduction and Background

This survey builds on previous work started in 2007 at University of Wisconsin Extension (Nath & Ralston-Berg, 2008; Ralston-Berg & Nath, 2008; Ralston-Berg & Nath, 2009). The Quality Matters (QM) program offers quality assurance through a research-based rubric for online course design. From an instructional design standpoint, questions arise about the student perspective. If the QM Rubric is based on academic research initiated most often by content experts or others in academia delivering online content, do online students – consumers of those courses – have a differing perspective on what makes a quality online course? Do students agree that items presented in the QM Rubric indicate quality? Are items in the QM Rubric perceived as contributors to student success?

Method

Data were collected through an online survey made available through a unique URL by a contact person at each participating institution. The URLs were delivered to students via email, a link posted on a CMS home page, or in an online course announcement. Data from each institution were then compiled into a cumulative dataset. Three datasets were gathered from 2010 to 2011.

Participants

Participants were currently enrolled or had taken online, for-credit courses and were over 18 years of age. Information here describes cumulative results of all datasets for a total online sample of N=3,160 students from 31 institutions in 22 states. Participants ranged in age from 18 to 65+ with the largest group being 26–44-year-olds. They represented 25 areas of study and a range of online experience from 1 to 9+ courses completed. Most participants were enrolled in cohort, for-credit online courses from a four-year institution. The majority were enrolled part time (two or more courses) or full time and reported being comfortable or very comfortable with technology.

Survey

The instrument contained QM items from the 2008–2010 Rubric converted to student-centered language, open response

[A]Penn State World Campus

questions about quality, and demographic information (Appendix A). Participants were asked to consider only the online course environment when rating each online course feature in terms of how valuable they thought it to be. Students rated each course characteristic on a four-point Likert scale as to how each item contributes to student success (i.e., 0=not at all important – does not contribute to my success; 1=important; 2=very important; and 3=essential – could not succeed without it).

Results

The cumulative mean and standard deviation were calculated for each survey item. This was then compared to the corresponding 2008–2010 and 2011–2013 QM Rubric item numbers and their QM-assigned point values. Participants found all survey items to be important. However, some survey items were rated differently when compared to 2008–2010 and 2011–2013 QM-assigned point values for each item. The results for each of the eight categories of QM Rubric items are listed in Tables 1 through 9.

Conclusions

All QM items were ranked important, although some items were ranked differently than QM-assigned values. Some QM-ranked "3" items were participant-ranked less than 2. Some QM-ranked "1" items were participant-ranked more than 2.

The results of this independent research were also incorporated into other works.

The QM Student Bill of Rights http://online.collin.edu/QM%20Bill%20of%20Rights%20for%20Online%20Learners%20with%20Preamble.pdf (Quality Matters, 2011) and accompanying video:

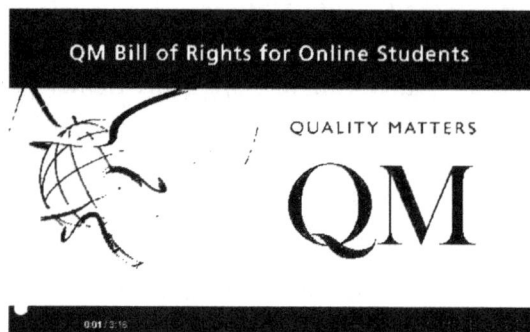

QM Bill of Rights for Online Students

QUALITY MATTERS

QM

0:01 / 3:16

http://www.youtube.com/watch?v=2mDbSvqBvR8

Joni Tornwall from the Ohio State University College of Nursing discussing QM Standards from the student perspective:

http://youtu.be/pzFYs8-IxN0

References

Nath, L. E., & Ralston-Berg, P. (2008). *Why Quality Matters matters: what students value.* Paper presented at the American Sociological Association Annual Meeting, Boston, MA.

Ralston-Berg, P., & Nath, L. (2008). What makes a quality online course? The student perspective. *Annual Conference on Teaching and Learning Proceedings.* Madison, WI.

Ralston-Berg, P., & Nath, L. (2009). What makes a quality online course? The student perspective. *Annual Conference on Teaching and Learning Proceedings.* Madison, WI.

Survey Item	Survey Mean	Survey SD	2008–2010 QM Rubric Item # and Points	2011–2013 QM Rubric Item # and Points
Clear instructions tell me how to get started and how to find various course components.	2.66	0.60	1.1 (3)	1.1 (3)
A statement introduces me to the purpose of the course and its components.	2.04	0.83	1.2 (3)	1.2 (3)
Etiquette (or "netiquette") guidelines for how to behave online are clearly stated.	1.43	0.93	1.3 (1)	1.3 (2)
The instructor introduces her- or himself.	1.91	0.87	1.4 (1)	1.7 (1)
I am asked to introduce myself to the class.	1.00	0.96	1.5 (1)	1.8 (1)
Minimum preparation or prerequisite knowledge I need to succeed in the course is clearly stated.	2.08	0.82	1.6 (1)	1.5 (1)
Minimum technical skills expected of me are clearly stated.	1.99	0.87	1.7 (1)	1.6 (1)

Table 1. Course Overview and Introduction

Survey Item	Survey Mean	Survey SD	2008–2010 QM Rubric Item # and Points	2011–2013 QM Rubric Item # and Points
The course learning objectives describe outcomes that I am able to achieve.	1.84	0.88	2.1 (3)	2.1 (3)
The module/unit learning objectives describe outcomes that I am able to achieve and are consistent with the course-level objectives. (For example, upon completing this lesson you will be able to…)	1.80	0.89	2.2 (3)	2.2 (3)
All learning objectives are clearly stated and written from my perspective.	1.83	0.90	2.3 (3)	2.3 (3)
Instructions on how to meet the learning objectives are adequate and stated clearly.	2.30	0.77	2.4 (3)	2.4 (3)
The learning objectives (my expected learning) are appropriate for the level of the course.	2.18	0.77	2.5 (2)	2.5 (3)

Table 2. Learning Objectives

Survey Item	Survey Mean	Survey SD	2008–2010 QM Rubric Item # and Points	2011–2013 QM Rubric Item # and Points
Assessments (quizzes, exams, papers, projects, etc.) measure the stated learning objectives and are consistent with course activities and resources.	2.48	0.66	3.1 (3)	3.1 (3)
The grading policy is stated clearly.	2.49	0.65	3.2 (3)	3.2 (3)
Criteria for how my work and participation will be evaluated are descriptive and specific. (For example, a grading rubric or list of expectations.)	2.52	0.64	3.3 (3)	3.3 (3)
Assessments (quizzes, exams, papers, projects, etc.) are appropriately timed within the length of the course, varied, and appropriate to the content being assessed.	2.49	0.65	3.4 (2)	3.4 (2)
"Self-check" or practice assignments are provided, and I am provided with timely feedback.	2.08	0.87	3.5 (2)	n/a

Table 3. Assessment and Measurement

Survey Item	Survey Mean	Survey SD	2008–2010 QM Rubric Item # and Points	2011–2013 QM Rubric Item # and Points
Instructional materials contribute to the achievement of the course and module/unit learning objectives.	2.29	0.72	4.1 (3)	4.1 (3)
The relationship between the instructional materials and the learning activities is clearly explained to me.	2.17	0.79	4.2 (3)	4.2 (3)
Instructional materials have sufficient breadth, depth, and currency for me to learn the subject.	2.32	0.73	4.3 (2)	n/a
All resources and materials used in the course are appropriately cited.	1.79	0.95	4.4 (1)	4.3 (2)

Table 4. Resources and Materials

Survey Item	Survey Mean	Survey SD	2008–2010 QM Rubric Item # and Points	2011–2013 QM Rubric Item # and Points
The learning activities promote the achievement of the stated course and module/unit learning objectives.	2.01	0.78	5.1 (3)	5.1 (3)
Learning activities encourage me to interact with content in the course.	1.96	0.82	5.2 (3)	5.2 (3)
Learning activities encourage me to interact with my instructor.	1.53	0.94	5.2 (3)	5.2 (3)
Learning activities encourage me to interact with other students.	1.24	0.98	5.2 (3)	5.2 (3)
Clear standards are set for instructor response (turn-around time for email, grade posting, etc.).	2.29	0.78	5.3 (2)	5.3 (3)
Clear standards are set for instructor availability (office hours, etc.)	2.16	0.83	5.3 (2)	5.3 (3)
Requirements for my interaction with the instructor, content, and other students are clearly explained.	2.35	0.76	5.4 (2)	5.4 (2)

Table 5. Learner Engagement

Survey Item	Survey Mean	Survey SD	2008–2010 QM Rubric Item # and Points	2011–2013 QM Rubric Item # and Points
The tools and media used are appropriate for the content being delivered.	2.17	0.77	6.1 (3)	n/a
The tools and media used support the achievement of the stated course and module/unit learning objectives.	2.05	0.83	6.1 (3)	6.1 (3)
Navigation throughout the online components of the course is logical, consistent, and efficient.	2.51	0.67	6.3 (3)	6.3 (3)
Technologies required for the course are readily available – provided or easily downloadable.	2.62	0.64	6.4 (2)	6.4 (2)
The course components are web-based or easily downloaded for use offline.	2.47	0.74	6.5 (1)	n/a
Instructions on how to access resources online are sufficient and easy to understand.	2.47	0.69	6.6 (1)	n/a
The course design takes full advantage of available tools and media.	2.06	0.85	6.7 (1)	n/a

Table 6. Course Technology

Survey Item	Survey Mean	Survey SD	2008–2010 QM Rubric Item # and Points	2011–2013 QM Rubric Item # and Points
Course includes or links to a clear description of the technical support offered to me.	2.05	0.83	7.1 (2)	7.1 (3)
Course includes or links to a clear explanation of how the institution's academic support system can assist me in effectively using the resources provided.	1.83	0.87	7.2 (2)	7.3 (2)
Course includes or links to a clear explanation of how the institution's student support services can help me reach my educational goals.	1.68	0.93	7.3 (1)	7.4 (1)
Course includes or links to tutorials and resources that answer basic questions related to research, writing, technology, etc.	1.75	0.92	7.4 (1)	n/a

Table 7. Learner Support

Survey Item	Survey Mean	Survey SD	2008–2010 QM Rubric Item # and Points	2011–2013 QM Rubric Item # and Points
Course is accessible to people with disabilities.	1.74	1.13	8.1 (3)	n/a
Course includes equivalent alternatives to audio and visual content.	1.65	1.06	8.2 (2)	8.2 (2)
Course includes web links that are self-describing and meaningful.	1.84	0.89	8.3 (2)	n/a
Course ensures screen readability.	2.32	0.83	8.4 (1)	n/a

Table 8. Accessibility

All survey items were compiled into one list to determine overall rank or value to participants. This provides a resource for instructional designers and course developers.

Table 9. All Survey Items in Order of Participant Rank

Survey Item	QM Rank	Survey Rank	SD
Clear instructions tell me how to get started and how to find various course components.	3	2.66	0.60
Technologies required for the course are readily available – provided or easily downloadable.	2	2.62	0.64
Criteria for how my work and participation will be evaluated are descriptive and specific. (For example, a grading rubric or list of expectations.)	3	2.52	0.64
Navigation throughout the online components of the course is logical, consistent, and efficient.	3	2.51	0.67
Assessments (quizzes, exams, papers, projects, etc.) are appropriately timed within the length of the course, varied, and appropriate to the content being assessed.	2	2.49	0.65
The grading policy is stated clearly.	3	2.49	0.65
Assessments (quizzes, exams, papers, projects, etc.) measure the stated learning objectives and are consistent with course activities and resources.	3	2.48	0.66
Instructions on how to access resources online are sufficient and easy to understand.	1	2.47	0.69
The course components are web-based or easily downloaded for use offline.	1	2.47	0.74
Requirements for my interaction with the instructor, content, and other students are clearly explained.	2	2.35	0.76
Instructional materials have sufficient breadth, depth, and currency for me to learn the subject.	2	2.32	0.73
Course ensures screen readability.	1	2.32	0.83
Instructions on how to meet the learning objectives are adequate and stated clearly.	3	2.30	0.77
Instructional materials contribute to the achievement of the course and module/unit learning objectives.	3	2.29	0.72
Clear standards are set for instructor response (turn-around time for email, grade posting, etc.).	2	2.29	0.78
The learning objectives (my expected learning) are appropriate for the level of the course.	2	2.18	0.77
The tools and media used are appropriate for the content being delivered.	3	2.17	0.77
The relationship between the instructional materials and the learning activities is clearly explained to me.	3	2.17	0.79

Clear standards are set for instructor availability (office hours, etc.)	2	2.16	0.83
"Self-check" or practice assignments are provided, and I am provided with timely feedback.	2	2.08	0.87
Minimum preparation or prerequisite knowledge I need to succeed in the course is clearly stated.	1	2.08	0.82
The course design takes full advantage of available tools and media.	1	2.06	0.85
Course includes or links to a clear description of the technical support offered to me.	2	2.05	0.83
The tools and media used support the achievement of the stated course and module/unit learning objectives.	3	2.05	0.83
A statement introduces me to the purpose of the course and its components.	3	2.04	0.83
The learning activities promote the achievement of the stated course and module/unit learning objectives.	3	2.01	0.78
Minimum technical skills expected of me are clearly stated.	1	1.99	0.87
Learning activities encourage me to interact with content in the course.	3	1.96	0.82
The instructor introduces her- or himself.	1	1.91	0.87
The course learning objectives describe outcomes that I am able to achieve.	3	1.84	0.88
Course includes web links that are self-describing and meaningful.	2	1.84	0.89
All learning objectives are clearly stated and written from my perspective.	3	1.83	0.90
Course includes or links to a clear explanation of how the institution's academic support system can assist me in effectively using the resources provided.	2	1.83	0.87
The module/unit learning objectives describe outcomes that I am able to achieve and are consistent with the course-level objectives. (For example, upon completing this lesson you will be able to…)	3	1.80	0.89
All resources and materials used in the course are appropriately cited.	1	1.79	0.95
Course includes or links to tutorials and resources that answer basic questions related to research, writing, technology, etc.	1	1.75	0.92
Course is accessible to people with disabilities.	3	1.74	1.13
Course includes or links to a clear explanation of how the institution's student support services can help me reach my educational goals.	1	1.68	0.93
Course includes equivalent alternatives to audio and visual content.	2	1.65	1.06
Learning activities encourage me to interact with my instructor.	3	1.53	0.94
Etiquette (or "netiquette") guidelines for how to behave online are clearly stated.	1	1.43	0.93
Learning activities encourage me to interact with other students.	3	1.24	0.98
I am asked to introduce myself to the class.	1	1.00	0.96

Survey Item	QM Rank	Participant Rank
Learning activities encourage me to interact with content in the course.	3	1.96
The course learning objectives describe outcomes that I am able to achieve.	3	1.84
All learning objectives are clearly stated and written from my perspective.	3	1.83
The module/unit learning objectives describe outcomes that I am able to achieve and are consistent with the course-level objectives. (For example, upon completing this lesson you will be able to…)	3	1.80
Course is accessible to people with disabilities.	3	1.74
Learning activities encourage me to interact with my instructor.	3	1.53
Learning activities encourage me to interact with other students.	3	1.24

Table 10. QM "3" Items Ranked <2 by Participants

Survey Item	QM Rank	Participant Rank
Instructions on how to access resources online are sufficient and easy to understand.	1	2.47
The course components are web-based or easily downloaded for use offline.	1	2.47
Course ensures screen readability.	1	2.32
Minimum preparation or prerequisite knowledge I need to succeed in the course is clearly stated.	1	2.08
The course design takes full advantage of available tools and media.	1	2.06

Table 11. QM "1" Items Ranked >2 by Participants

www.ingramcontent.com/pod-product-compliance
Lightning Source LLC
LaVergne TN
LVHW061327060426
835511LV00012B/1905

www.ingramcontent.com/pod-product-compliance
Lightning Source LLC
LaVergne TN
LVHW061327060426
835511LV00012B/1894